BREAKING THE CYCLE
OF
Defeat

DEFEAT TO VICTORY

RAMESH C KOUNDAL

Breaking The Cycle of Defeat

Publisher: Inkscribe Media Pvt. Ltd

ISBN Number: 978-1-966421-33-7

Contents

Introduction

Romans 8:37 – "In all these things we are more than conquerors through him who loved us."

As the narrative draws to a close, the essence of transformation becomes the cornerstone of our understanding. The path from defeat to victory is not merely a journey of overcoming obstacles but a profound metamorphosis of the mind and spirit. The trials that once seemed insurmountable have now become the very crucibles that forged resilience and strength. Through the lens of adversity, the characters have discovered that true victory does not lie in the absence of challenges but in the unwavering faith and tenacity to rise above them. In the tapestry of life, each thread of struggle has been woven into a pattern of triumph, creating a fabric that is both beautiful and enduring. The lessons learnt are not just personal victories but universal truths that resonate with all who seek to break free from the chains of defeat. By embracing the power of faith, the characters have tapped into an inner reservoir of strength, allowing them to navigate the complexities of life with grace and confidence. This transformation is a testament to the indomitable spirit that resides within us all, urging us to face our fears and conquer them with courage and hope. As the final chapter closes, it leaves us with a profound sense of empowerment, inspiring us to embark on our own paths to victory. The cycle of defeat is broken, and in its place, a new cycle of hope and possibility emerges, lighting the way for those who dare to believe in the power of their dreams.

My prayers are that the Lord will take you from defeat to victory, which He has achieved for you already in Christ Jesus, and give you insights to apply in your life.

1

Understanding the Cycle of Defeat

Recognising the Patterns

In the quest to overcome persistent patterns of defeat, the first essential step is to identify and understand the underlying patterns that perpetuate this cycle. Recognising these patterns involves an introspective look at the circumstances and responses that lead to a feeling of defeat. This process begins with acknowledging that many of these patterns are not random but are orchestrated through various strategies that aim to keep individuals trapped in a cycle of negativity and self-doubt through deception by the devil.

One common pattern is the tendency to focus excessively on negative circumstances, which can lead to a mindset dominated by stress and anxiety. When faced with challenging situations, it is natural to feel overwhelmed. However, dwelling on these circumstances without seeking a constructive way forward can reinforce feelings of helplessness. This is a strategy often exploited by negative forces to keep individuals from realising their full potential.

To break free from this cycle, it is crucial to shift focus away from the circumstances themselves and instead concentrate on the possibilities for overcoming them. This requires a deliberate change in mindset, where one actively chooses to view challenges as opportunities for growth rather than insurmountable obstacles. One effective method is to replace stress with peace by consciously setting the mind on positive outcomes and trusting in sovereign God or inner strength through the Holy Spirit to guide the way. As mentioned in Philippians 4:6-7, "Be anxious for nothing, but in everything by prayer and supplication, with thanksgiving, let your requests be made known to God; and the peace of God, which surpasses all understanding, will guard your hearts and minds through Christ Jesus."

Another aspect of recognising patterns involves understanding the role of fear and doubt in perpetuating defeat. Fear is a spirit (2 Timotheos 1:7) and can be a powerful inhibitor, preventing individuals from taking necessary actions to change their situation. Similarly, doubt can erode confidence, making it difficult to believe in the possibility of success. By identifying moments when fear and doubt take hold, individuals can begin to develop strategies to counteract these feelings, such as affirmations of faith or positive self-talk. Psalm 50:15 says that you can let doubt, fear, and worry overtake you, or you can call upon the Lord. God has promised that if you call upon Him, He will deliver you. The deliverance may not look exactly like you expect, but you can be 100% sure that He will help you.

Moreover, it is essential to understand that these patterns are not just mental but can manifest in physical and emotional responses. Stress, for instance, can lead to physical symptoms like fatigue and tension, which further perpetuate the cycle of defeat. In the Bible, people experiencing intense fear are often described as trembling, like when the disciples were "greatly afraid" and "trembled" in the presence of Jesus on the Sea of Galilee (Mark 4:41). Worry and anxiety stemming from doubt can lead to disrupted sleep, as mentioned in Psalm 13:2, where the psalmist says, "I cannot sleep because of grief."

Recognising these signs early can help individuals take proactive steps to manage stress, such as through relaxation techniques, exercise, or seeking support from others, but especially through Bible words such as "Cast all your anxiety on him because he cares for you." (1 Peter 5:7).

Ultimately, recognising the patterns that lead to defeat is about becoming aware of the strategies that work against personal growth and finding ways to counteract them. This involves a combination of self-awareness, mental resilience, and a willingness to seek new perspectives. "Be strong and courageous. Do not be afraid; do not be discouraged, for the Lord your God will be with you wherever you go." (Joshua 1:9).

"The Lord is my light and my salvation—whom shall I fear? The Lord is the stronghold of my life—of whom shall I be afraid?" (Psalm 27:1). By doing so, individuals can begin to break free from the cycle of defeat and move towards a more empowered and victorious way of living.

Understanding these patterns is the foundation upon which one can build a life that is not only free from defeat but is also rich with potential and possibility. 1 Corinthians 15:57 - But thanks be to God, who gives us the victory through our Lord Jesus Christ.

The Role of Circumstances

Circumstances play a pivotal role in shaping our experiences and responses, often becoming the battleground where cycles of defeat are either perpetuated or broken. Recognising the influence of circumstances is crucial in understanding how to navigate life's challenges effectively. In the context of spiritual and personal growth, circumstances are not just random occurrences but are seen as opportunities for growth and testing of faith.

In Romans 6:5-10 the apostle Paul expounds the truth that each believer is united with Christ in His total victory over sin, death and Satan. This is an infallible truth upon which each believer is responsible to stand. Sin and Satan cannot rule over a dead person.

Sin cannot master and put into slavery a person who is now "alive unto God" because of our union with Christ in His resurrection. That is an infallible, unchanging truth upon which we are meant to stand regardless of experience.

So let us not trust your experiences of defeat but the truth, the word of God, which can set you free.

Understanding that circumstances are governed by a higher purpose can transform how individuals perceive and react to them. It is emphasized that God is ultimately in control of all situations, and while Satan may use circumstances to attempt to defeat and discourage, these same situations can be transformed into opportunities for victory and personal development. Genesis 50:20 says that "But as for you, you meant evil against me; but God meant it for good, in order to bring it about as it is this day, to save many people alive." The belief is that God allows certain challenges to refine, strengthen, and mature individuals, ensuring that they emerge from trials more resilient and steadfast, as mentioned in Romans 8:28. "And we know that all things work together for good to those who love God, to those who are the called according to His purpose."

A key aspect of overcoming negative circumstances is maintaining a perspective that focuses not on the problems themselves but on the potential for growth and victory through them. This perspective shift is vital in breaking the cycle of defeat that often accompanies difficult situations. By understanding that with every challenge comes a provision for victory, individuals can face their trials with confidence and hope.

Isaiah 41:10 says, "Fear not, for I am with you; be not dismayed, for I am your God. I will strengthen you; yes, I will help you. I will uphold you with My righteous right hand."

The writings highlight the importance of faith and resilience in the face of adversity. It is through faith that one can see beyond the immediate discomfort of a situation and trust in a greater plan. Psalm 46:1 says, "God is our refuge and strength, always ready to help in times of trouble. So, we will not fear when earthquakes come and the mountains crumble into the sea."

This trust is not passive but requires active engagement in faith practices, such as prayer and reflection, to align one's mindset with the promises of victory and strength that can be obtained through God's promise. Hebrews 10:22-23 also says, "Let us draw near with a true heart in full assurance of faith, having our hearts sprinkled from an evil conscience and our bodies washed with pure water. Let us hold fast the confession of our hope without wavering, for He who promised is faithful." In doing so, individuals can resist the temptation to succumb to despair and instead find strength in the knowledge that every circumstance is an opportunity for God to demonstrate His power and faithfulness.

Moreover, the role of circumstances is not just about personal growth but also about the impact on others. As individuals navigate their challenges with faith and resilience, they become testimonies of hope and encouragement to those around them. This communal aspect of overcoming circumstances underscores the interconnectedness of personal victories with the broader community.

In summary, the role of circumstances in the cycle of defeat is significant. We are sometimes led by the experience of defeat and circumstances by the devil, making us think that prayers and proclaiming the word of God are not working in our lives, or we are made to think sometimes that my case situation is unique and difficult beyond what anyone else has experienced. The secret of the enemy's strength in that case is that we assign the devil an invincible role in our lives, and he is too happy to assume that. By understanding and embracing the divine purpose behind every challenge, individuals can transform potential defeats into victories. This transformation is facilitated by a steadfast faith in God's control and purpose, an active engagement in spiritual practices, and a focus on the potential for growth and impact on others. Through this understanding, the cycle of defeat can be broken, paving the way for a life characterised by victory and fulfilment.

Impact on Mind and Spirit

The impact of circumstances on the mind and spirit is profound, often serving as a battleground where defeat or victory is determined. The mind is a primary target in the cycle of defeat, where stress, worry, and doubt can take root if not actively resisted. When the mind is filled with these negative emotions, it becomes susceptible to further attacks, leading to a weakened spirit. 2 Corinthians 10:4-5:

"For the weapons of our warfare are not carnal, but mighty through God to the pulling down of strongholds, casting down imaginations and every high thing that exalts itself against the knowledge of God, and bringing every thought into captivity to the obedience of Christ." This verse directly speaks to the spiritual warfare that takes place in our minds, where we are called to take our thoughts captive and align them with Christ's will. This state can paralyse faith, making it difficult to believe in the promises and truths that offer liberation from such cycles. The mind's renewal is essential (Romans 12:2) to breaking free from the cycle of defeat. By focusing on positive thoughts and truths, individuals can resist the negative influences that seek to dominate their spirit, as we are more than conquerors in Him who loved us (Romans 8:37). This renewal involves an active decision to replace stress with peace, a peace that is grounded in faith and trust in God's sovereign benevolent plan. The spirit, when fortified by a peaceful mind, gains strength to withstand trials and tribulations that life may present by trusting God. Psalm 46:10: "Be still and know that I am God." The transformation of the mind, therefore, is not merely about avoiding negative thoughts but about cultivating a mindset that sees beyond current circumstances to the potential for growth and victory. The spirit thrives when the mind is aligned with positive affirmations and truths, enabling individuals to rise above the challenges they face. This alignment fosters resilience, an essential quality that empowers individuals to persist in the face of adversity, knowing that their trials are not the end but a pathway to greater strength and wisdom. James 1:2-4: "Consider it pure joy, my brothers and sisters, whenever you face trials of many kinds, because you know that the testing of your faith produces perseverance. Let perseverance finish its work so that you may be mature and complete, not lacking anything." The spirit, once free from the chains of doubt and fear, can soar to new heights of understanding and purpose, creating a life pattern that is characterised not by defeat but by continuous growth and fulfilment. Such a mindset shift (You will keep in perfect peace those whose minds are steadfast because they trust in you. Isaiah 26:3) is crucial in transforming the cycle of defeat into a cycle of victory, enabling individuals to live life with a renewed sense of purpose and joy. This shift in perspective allows the individual to view challenges not as insurmountable obstacles but as opportunities for personal and spiritual development. In this way, the mind (the soul called mind, will and emotions) and spirit work in harmony, creating a life that is not only resilient in the face of adversity but also rich in meaning and fulfilment. The journey to breaking the cycle of defeat is thus a profound transformation of both mind and spirit, leading to a life that is victorious and free.

Breaking the Chains

In the pursuit of overcoming life's challenges, it is essential to recognise the strategies that often bind individuals in a cycle of defeat. One of the most pervasive tactics is the manipulation of circumstances to instill fear, doubt, and worry. This psychological grip can lead to a state of paralysis, where faith is choked, and the ability to trust in positive outcomes diminishes. To effectively break these chains, one must adopt a proactive approach that centres on shifting focus from the overwhelming nature of current situations to the empowering truths of a higher purpose in Christ and divine support from Him.

The first step in dismantling these chains is to cultivate a mindset that refuses to be dominated by negative circumstances. This involves a conscious decision to replace thoughts of fear and worry with peace and assurance. The word of God promises in Philippians 4:6-7: "Do not be anxious about anything, but in everything by prayer and supplication with thanksgiving let your requests be made known to God. And the peace of God, which surpasses all understanding, will guard your hearts and your minds in Christ Jesus."

By redirecting focus from the chaos of external situations to the stability provided by spiritual truths, individuals can begin to experience a profound sense of calm. Psalm 34:17 "The righteous cry out, and the Lord hears and delivers them out of all their troubles." Deliverance brings peace, and this peace is not merely the absence of conflict but a deep-seated confidence in the presence and promises found in scripture.

Moreover, it is crucial to understand that the very circumstances designed to defeat can be transformed into opportunities for growth and victory, as Romans 8:28 conveys that "And we know that all things work together for good to those who love God, to those who are the called according to His purpose." Each challenge presents a choice: to succumb to the pressure or to stand firm in faith. By viewing trials as a means to strengthen character and deepen resilience (Roman 5:3-5), individuals can navigate through adversity with a sense of purpose and determination. This perspective shift is vital in breaking free from the cycle of defeat, as it empowers individuals to see beyond immediate hardships and envision a future filled with potential and promise.

Another critical aspect of breaking the chains is the active resistance against the forces that seek to undermine confidence and faith. This involves a strategic use of spiritual tools and principles, such as prayer, meditation, and the affirmation of positive truths found in relevant Bible verses. Ephesians 4:23: "To be made new in the attitude of your minds." Colossians 3:2: "Set your minds on things that are above, not on things that are on earth." By engaging in these practices, individuals can fortify their minds against the onslaught of negative thoughts and emotions that threaten to derail their progress. John 8:32 "And you will know the truth, and the truth will make you free." It is through this disciplined focus on spiritual truths that one can maintain clarity and direction amidst life's storms.

Finally, the journey to breaking these chains is not one that is undertaken alone. It is supported by a community of like-minded individuals, mature believers/Pastors who offer encouragement, share insights, and provide accountability. This communal aspect is vital, as it reinforces the belief that while challenges are personal, the strength to overcome them is collective. By surrounding oneself with a network of support, individuals can draw on the collective wisdom and experience of others, further bolstering their resolve to live in victory.

In essence, breaking the chains of defeat involves a holistic approach that combines mental fortitude, spiritual grounding in the word of God, and communal support.

2 Corinthians 10:3-6 "For though we walk in the flesh, we do not war according to the flesh. For the weapons of

our warfare are not carnal but mighty in God for pulling down strongholds, casting down arguments and every high thing that exalts itself against the knowledge of God, bringing every thought into captivity to the obedience of Christ, and being ready to punish all disobedience when your obedience is fulfilled.

The concept of "walking in victory" with the support of like-minded believers is strongly reflected in the Bible, particularly in the idea of Christian community and the power of collective faith.

Philippians 2:1-2 says, "Therefore if you have any encouragement from being united with Christ, if any comfort from his love, if any common sharing in the Spirit, if any tenderness and compassion, then make my joy complete by being like-minded, having the same love, being one in spirit and of one mind."

Romans 12:10: "Be devoted to one another in love. Honour one another above yourselves."

Hebrews 10:24-25: "And let us consider how we may spur one another on toward love and good deeds, not giving up meeting together, as some are in the habit of doing, but encouraging one another—and all the more as you see the Day approaching."

How this relates to "walking in victory":

Strength in Numbers: -

When believers come together with a shared faith and purpose, they can offer mutual support and encouragement, which empowers them to overcome challenges and "walk in victory" over life's difficulties. Accountability: -

A community of like-minded believers can hold each other accountable to live according to God's word, helping to maintain a strong spiritual walk.

Shared Faith: -

By openly sharing their faith and experiences, believers can strengthen each other's convictions and deepen their understanding of God's power.

By embracing these elements, individuals can transcend the limitations imposed by their circumstances and step into a life characterised by freedom, purpose, and fulfilment.

2

Satan's Strategies Revealed

Using Circumstances Against You

The adversary, Satan, seeks to exploit your circumstances, aiming to ensnare you in a relentless cycle of defeat. His strategy is to use the very fabric of your daily life to undermine your spirit, hoping to drain your mental and physical resilience. It is crucial to understand that while Satan's attacks can feel overwhelming, they are not insurmountable. His ultimate goal is to keep you preoccupied with stress, fear, and doubt, effectively paralysing your faith and hindering your ability to realise the victory that God has prepared for you. Satan is occupying an invincible role in our lives by deceiving us in our experience of battle, and in our experience of defeat, we are letting him reign in our lives. Many are deceived in this way.

In every aspect of life—whether it be health, finances, relationships, or career—Satan attempts to sow seeds of doubt and despair. He may try to bind your finances, bring sickness into your life, or cause rifts in your family. Through these challenges, he hopes to wear you down so that you may feel defeated and ready to surrender. Yet, it is vital to remember that no circumstance, no matter how dire, can ultimately defeat you if you remain steadfast in faith (1 Corinthians 16:13).

God has not promised a life free from trials, but He has assured us victory in every difficult circumstance. The key to overcoming these trials lies in recognising that God is in control of every situation. He places a limit on what Satan can do, ensuring that you are never tested beyond what you can bear. With every trial, God provides a way of escape, a path to triumph that strengthens your faith and builds endurance. This concept is directly linked to the verse 1 Corinthians 10:13, which says, "No temptation has overtaken you that is not common to man. God is faithful, and he will not let you be tempted beyond your ability, but with the temptation he will also provide the way of escape, that you may be able to endure it."

To break the cycle of defeat, it is essential to shift your focus from the circumstances to the promises of God, which can give victory. Truth is not there in our experience but in the word of God, which says, "And you will know the truth, and the truth will set you free," is a quote from the Bible, John 8:32. This involves a conscious decision to refuse to dwell on the problems and instead fix your eyes on Jesus and His Word. By doing so, you can reclaim your peace and joy, even in the midst of adversity. Releasing your faith, you must stand firm in the belief that God will turn every negative situation into an opportunity for growth and victory.

Moreover, it is important to actively resist Satan's attempts to sow doubt and fear. This resistance is not passive; it requires you to take up spiritual weapons, cast out every thought of fear and doubt in the name of Jesus, and declare God's promises over your life. 2 Corinthians 10:3-4 "For though we walk in the flesh, we do not war according to the flesh. For the weapons of our warfare are not [a]carnal but mighty in God for pulling down strongholds, casting down arguments and every high thing that exalts itself against the knowledge of God, bringing every thought into captivity to the obedience of Christ." As you engage in this spiritual battle, remember that victory is not achieved through your strength but through the power of God working within you.

Ultimately, God uses the circumstances that Satan intends for harm to perfect and strengthen you. Each test becomes a stepping stone towards spiritual maturity, bringing you to a place where you are complete, lacking nothing.

Satan Will Not Win

Those are some of Satan's designs. The path to victory in this warfare is to hold fast to Christ, who has already dealt the decisive blow.

➤ 1 John 3:8: "The Son of God appeared to destroy the works of the devil."

➤ Hebrews 2:14: "Christ took on human nature that through death he might destroy him who has the power of death, that is, the devil."

> ➤ Colossians 2:15: "God disarmed the principalities and powers and made a public example of them, triumphing over them in him." In other words, the decisive blow was struck at Calvary.

> ➤ Mark 3:27: "No one can enter a strong man's house and plunder his goods unless he first binds the strong man."

> ➤ Revelation 20:10 says one day the warfare will be over: "The devil . . . [will be] thrown into the lake of fire and brimstone . . . and will be tormented day and night forever and ever." (See Matthew 8:29; 25:41)

By standing firm in this knowledge and exercising unwavering faith, you can transform every trial into a testimony of God's faithfulness and power, breaking the cycle of defeat and stepping into a cycle of victory.

Instilling Fear and Doubt

The narrative of instilling fear and doubt begins with the disciples caught in a violent storm (Matthew 8:23-27, Mark 4:35-41, and Luke 8:22-25), a metaphor for life's overwhelming challenges. The storm symbolises the external pressures that Satan uses to incite fear and doubt, aiming to distract from God's presence and promises. The disciples, despite witnessing Jesus' miracles, let the storm overshadow their faith, illustrating how easily circumstances can cloud judgement and lead to spiritual blindness. This scenario highlights the core of Satan's strategy: to divert focus from divine assurance to temporal turmoil.

In this struggle, fear becomes a tool that Satan wields with precision. It is designed to grip the mind, constricting the ability to trust in God's power and love. This fear is not merely an emotion but a spirit & spiritual weapon that distorts reality, making challenges appear insurmountable. Doubt, its companion, creeps in to question God's intentions and promises, further destabilising faith. The disciples' panic is a testament to how fear and doubt can paralyse spiritual action, preventing the manifestation of faith in action.

Satan's strategy is meticulous, seeking to exploit every moment of weakness. The more one focuses on the storm—the challenges and uncertainties—the more faith is marginalised. This focus on circumstances rather than the divine leads to a cycle of defeat, where worry and anxiety reign. It is a vicious cycle that Satan perpetuates, knowing that a mind preoccupied with fear cannot rest in God's peace. The disciples' experience serves as a cautionary tale of how easily faith can be overshadowed by fear when the focus shifts from God to the problem at hand.

We know that our number one enemy is Satan. He is a "liar and the father of lies" (John 8:44). He is "your enemy [who] prowls around like a roaring lion looking for someone to devour" (1 Peter 5:8). He is "the accuser of the brethren, who accuses them before our God day and night" (Revelation 12:10); and because he wants to steal souls from the Lord, Satan uses our weaknesses against us in order to cause us to sin, in hopes that we will stray from God and continue to live in sin.

Breaking this cycle requires a conscious shift in focus. It demands a deliberate act of will to cast all worries onto God, recognising His sovereignty and care. This act is not passive but involves actively resisting the temptation to dwell on fears and doubts. It requires a steadfast belief in God's promises, a refusal to let circumstances dictate spiritual reality. By doing so, one can experience the peace that Jesus exemplified, even amidst chaos. Remember this: if you give Satan even an inch, he will think he can rule your life and will try anything to do so.

The narrative encourages believers to recognise and resist Satan's tactics. It calls for a faith that is not swayed by external storms but anchored in the assurance of God's unchanging word.

Claim God's promises for your life and hold on to what God says. To have a hopeful outlook is possible when we shift our perspective on how God sees things and His promises, rather than on the storm we might be facing. As you meditate on God's promises found in His unchanging Word, you and your attitude will be grounded. "It is impossible for God to lie" (Hebrews 6)

When you think, "I've lost hope"

God says, "Hold on to My hope" (Psalms 62:5).

When you think, "It is impossible",

God says, "All things are possible with Me" (Luke 18:27).

When you think, "I cannot do it"

God says, "You can all do all things through Christ" (Philippians 4:13).

When you think, "Nothing good can come out of this."

God says, "I know how to bring good out of this" (Romans 8:28).

When you think, "I can't meet all my needs"

God says, "I can meet all your needs" (Philippians 4:19).

Hope in God and His power: -

We are called to hope. Hope is not wishful thinking or imagining things. We can put our hope and trust in the character of God and His love for us. Pray, rely on Him and expect His perfect will and timing to see His promise come through.

"Why are you downcast? O my soul? Why so disturbed within me? Put our hope in God, for I will yet praise Him, my Saviour and my God" (Psalm 42:5).

This faith is proactive, taking deliberate steps to reject fear and embrace divine peace. It involves continuously redirecting focus from the storm to the Saviour Jesus Christ, maintaining a perspective that sees beyond the immediate to the eternal.

Ultimately, instilling fear and doubt is about control—about shifting one's allegiance from God to the circumstances. By understanding this strategy, believers can guard against it, ensuring that their faith remains vibrant and unyielding. The call to action is clear: keep eyes on Jesus, trust in His promises, and let His peace reign, breaking the cycle of defeat that Satan seeks to impose.

Paralysed with Worry

Fear is right when it is reverence toward God because of his holiness (Isa 8:13), and care is good when showing concern for others (1 Co 12:25; 2 Co 11:28). But worry is always wrong, for it paralyses active faith in your life. When you worry, you assume responsibility for things you were never intended to handle.

Worry is a formidable force that can stifle one's ability to live a fulfilling and victorious life. It acts as a barrier, inhibiting the flow of faith and rendering the Word of God ineffective. This state of mind is not just a passive experience but an active strategy used by negative forces to keep individuals trapped in a cycle of defeat. When one's mind is consumed by worry, fear, and doubt, it becomes paralysed, unable to function with clarity and purpose. This paralysis prevents one from receiving the blessings and promises that are rightfully theirs.

The process begins subtly, as worry creeps in through various circumstances—whether they be financial troubles, health issues, or personal relationships. These worries occupy the mind, creating a constant state of anxiety and stress. The mind becomes a battlefield where negative thoughts and fears are given space to grow, overshadowing any positive affirmations or beliefs. This mental clutter chokes the Word, making it unfruitful and ineffective in one's life.

Worrying is harmful. Worry is a choking, harmful emotion that saps your energy and elevates human strength and ingenuity above God's strength and his purposeful plan. Sources of worry include change, lack of understanding and lack of control over your life. Worry opens the door to worldliness, that is, preoccupation with the things of this life. Though the children of Israel had watched God split open the Red Sea to deliver them from Egypt, they could not believe he would provide water in the desert to meet their needs.

Worry is the opposite of faith, suggesting that God cannot be trusted to take care of you or to provide what you need. Worry causes fear to crowd out faith. Thus, in the final reckoning, "the cowardly" are listed alongside the "unbelieving" (Rev 21:8). Linking worry with unbelief, Scripture gives direction for a return to full faith. The road from worry to faith begins with recognition that worry is sin and confession of lack of faith (Ps 139:23), continues with deliverance (Ps 34:4), and finally ends with the assurance that absolutely nothing can separate you from the love of God, who is the great I am (Ro 8:35; Ex 3:14–15).

To overcome this paralysing worry, it is essential to recognise it as a deliberate strategy of the devil designed to distract and destabilise. Awareness of this tactic is the first step in dismantling its hold. Once recognised, one must actively work to shift focus away from the circumstances that fuel worry. This involves a conscious effort to redirect thoughts towards faith and trust in divine promises. By doing so, individuals can reclaim their mental space and prevent worry from taking root.

Practical steps include taking one's eyes off the immediate problems and instead focusing on solutions and positive outcomes through the word of God, as the word of God says in Philippians 4:6-7. "Do not be anxious about anything, but in every situation, by prayer and petition, with thanksgiving, present your requests to God. And the peace of God, which transcends all understanding, will guard your hearts and your minds in Christ Jesus." This shift in perspective allows for a release of faith, enabling individuals to trust sovereign God and the fulfilment of His promises. It is also crucial to resist the temptation to dwell on negative thoughts, as this only serves to strengthen worry's grip.

2 Corinthians 10:3-5 says, "For though we live in the world, we do not wage war as the world does. The weapons we fight with are not the weapons of the world. On the contrary, they have divine power to demolish strongholds. We demolish arguments and every pretension that sets itself up against the knowledge of God, and we take captive every thought to make it obedient to Christ." Hence, one should cast out these thoughts by the word of God as quoted above, declaring their intent to live free from fear and doubt.

Moreover, it is important to reinforce the mind with positive affirmations and truths that counteract worry. Psalm 23:4:

"Even though I walk through the valley of the shadow of death, I will fear no evil, for you are with me; your rod and your staff, they comfort me." Isaiah 41:10: "So do not fear, for I am with you; do not be dismayed, for I am your God. I will strengthen you and help you; I will uphold you with my righteous right hand." John 14:27: "Peace I leave with you; my peace I give you. I do not give to you as the world gives. Do not let your hearts be troubled and do not be afraid." Fear brings worry.

Engaging in regular meditation or reflection on these truths can help solidify them in one's consciousness, providing a buffer against the infiltration of worry. 1 Peter 5:7 "Casting all your care upon Him, for He cares for you." By filling the mind with faith and confidence in these words of God, an individual can create a mental environment where worry cannot thrive.

Ultimately, breaking free from the paralysis of worry requires a commitment to live in victory rather than defeat. It demands a proactive approach to mental and spiritual well-being, where one consistently chooses faith over fear by declaring the following verse with your mouth.

Deuteronomy 31:6 "Be strong and of good courage; do not fear nor be afraid of them, for the Lord your God, He is the One who goes with you. He will not leave you nor forsake you."

Psalm 34:4 "I sought the Lord, and He heard me.

And delivered me from all my fears."

Psalm 23:4 Yea, though I walk through the valley of the shadow of death, I will fear no evil, for You are with me; Your rod and Your staff, they comfort me.

Isaiah 41:10 "Fear not, for I am with you; be not dismayed, for I am your God. I will strengthen you; yes, I will help you. I will uphold you with My righteous right hand."

As individuals learn to cast their worries by putting their trust in God's word as mentioned above and embrace a mindset of trust and belief, they open themselves up to receiving the full abundance of life's blessings. In doing so, they not only break the cycle of defeat but also set the stage for a life of peace and prosperity.

The Power of Faith

1 John 5:4 "For whatever is born of God overcomes the world. And this is the victory that has overcome the world—our faith." Faith is a powerful force that can break the cycle of defeat in our lives. It requires a steadfast belief in God's promises and the ability to trust Him completely, even when circumstances seem overwhelming. The essence of faith lies in its capacity to transcend the visible and the tangible, allowing individuals to anchor their hope in the unseen yet assured promises of God. This unwavering belief is not merely passive; it is active and dynamic, demanding a

conscious decision to trust in God's word and His intentions for our lives. We can learn from Abraham, as mentioned in Romans 4:20, which says, "He did not waver at the promise of God through unbelief but was strengthened in faith, giving glory to God." Like this, it involves casting all worries and concerns upon Him, a process that necessitates a deliberate act of will. By doing so, individuals can experience a profound peace that guards their hearts and minds, shielding them from the debilitating effects of anxiety and fear as mentioned in Philippians 4:6-7. " Be anxious for nothing, but in everything by prayer and supplication, with thanksgiving, let your requests be made known to God; and the peace of God, which surpasses all understanding, will guard your hearts and minds through Christ Jesus." This divine peace is not a fleeting emotion but a stable state of being that enables believers to face their circumstances with confidence and assurance. Satan's strategy often involves instilling doubt and worry, which can choke the word of God in our hearts and render it ineffective. To counteract this, individuals must actively resist these negative thoughts and replace them with affirmations of faith (2 Corinthians 10:5). The Bible illustrates the power of faith through numerous accounts where individuals overcame insurmountable odds by trusting in God's promises. These stories serve as a testament to the transformative power of faith, encouraging believers to remain steadfast and unyielding in their trust in God. Faith is not blind optimism; it is rooted in the knowledge and understanding of God's nature and his unwavering commitment to His children. Bible verses about faith include Hebrews 11:1, Ephesians 2:8, and Proverbs

3:5, which describe faith as a trust in God's character and promises. Faith is not blind belief but rather an active choice to trust in God.

It is this understanding that empowers believers to stand firm in the face of adversity, knowing that their faith will ultimately lead to victory. The journey of faith is not without challenges, but it is through these trials that faith is strengthened and refined. James 1:2-4: James tells us to consider trials as pure joy because they produce perseverance.

As individuals continue to exercise their faith, they grow in spiritual maturity, becoming more resilient and capable of overcoming the obstacles that life presents. The power of faith lies in its ability to transform defeat into victory, despair into hope, and fear into courage. By embracing faith, individuals can break free from the cycle of defeat and enter into a cycle of victory, where they live in the fullness of God's promises and experience His abundant blessings. The Bible includes several verses that discuss overcoming fear and anxiety through faith, including Isaiah 41:10, Hebrews 11:1, and 2 Timothy 1:7. This transformative power is available to all who choose to believe and trust in God's word, making faith an indispensable tool in the journey towards spiritual growth and fulfilment.

3

The Power of God's Word

Faith in Action

The concept of 'Faith in Action' revolves around the idea that faith is not passive but an active, living force that manifests through our actions and decisions. James 2:17-18 states that "faith by itself, if it is not accompanied by action, is dead". In the context of overcoming life's challenges, faith becomes a powerful tool when it is translated into action. This chapter delves into how individuals can harness their faith to break free from cycles of defeat and enter a realm of victory.

Faith in action begins with a mindset that refuses to be overwhelmed by circumstances. It involves acknowledging that while challenges are inevitable, they are not insurmountable. By focusing on the positive outcomes that faith can bring, individuals can change their perspective from one of defeat to one of potential victory. This shift in mindset is crucial as it lays the groundwork for actionable steps towards overcoming difficulties.

An essential aspect of faith in action is the understanding that it requires perseverance. Life's challenges often test the limits of one's endurance and patience. However, through faith, individuals find the strength to persevere, knowing that each step taken in faith brings them closer to their breakthrough. This perseverance is not a passive waiting but an active engagement with life's challenges, armed with the belief that victory is possible.

Philippians 4:13 says, "I can do all things through Christ who strengthens me." It's a well-known verse in the Bible, but it's often misunderstood and misused. This verse reminds us that we can trust in Christ's strength during trials or struggles.

Furthermore, faith in action involves taking practical steps that align with one's beliefs. This means setting goals, making plans, and executing them with determination and trust in a higher power. It's about making informed decisions that reflect one's values and beliefs, even when the path is fraught with uncertainty. By doing so, individuals demonstrate their faith not just through words, but through their deeds.

Additionally, faith in action is about resilience. It is about rising after every fall, learning from failures, and continuing to push forward. This resilience is fuelled by the belief that setbacks are temporary and that perseverance will eventually lead to success. Faith provides the assurance that despite the current circumstances, there is hope and a promise of a better future.

Moreover, faith in action often involves community and support. Engaging with others who share similar beliefs can provide encouragement and strength. Hebrews 10:25 states, "not forsaking the assembling of ourselves together, as is the manner of some, but encouraging one another—and all the more as you see the Day approaching." It urges Christians to not abandon their gatherings for worship and fellowship but to encourage each other, especially as the return of Christ draws near. The collective power of shared faith can be a significant source of inspiration and motivation, helping individuals to stay committed to their path of victory.

Finally, faith in action is about trusting in a higher purpose. It is about believing that there is a reason for every challenge and that each experience is an opportunity for growth and development. This belief empowers individuals to face their trials with courage and optimism, knowing that their journey has a purpose and that they are being guided towards a greater good.

As God spoke to Joshua in Joshua 1:9, "Have I not commanded you? Be strong and courageous. Do not be afraid; do not be discouraged, for the Lord your God will be with you wherever you go."

In essence, faith in action is about turning belief into tangible outcomes. It is about living out one's faith through deliberate actions that reflect a deep trust in the positive power of faith. By doing so, individuals can break free from cycles of defeat and step into a life of victory and fulfilment.

Promises That Endure

In the midst of life's challenges, the assurance of enduring promises provides a beacon of hope and strength. In Matthew 24:13 Jesus said, "But he who endures to the end shall be saved." Isaiah 40:31 says, "But those who hope in the Lord will renew their strength. They will soar on wings like eagles; they will run and not grow weary; they will walk and not be faint." This verse promises renewed strength and endurance for those who trust in God, even when faced with exhaustion or challenges. These promises, deeply rooted in faith, serve as a reminder that no trial is insurmountable. A central theme is the understanding that while adversities are inevitable, they are not without purpose. Each challenge is an opportunity to witness the unfolding of divine promises that assure victory over defeat. The notion of being tested is not to imply abandonment but rather to highlight the strength and resilience that is cultivated through perseverance. Just as gold is refined through fire, so too is faith strengthened through trials.

In this context, the promises of God in Matthew 10:22 and 24:13, which say to endure, are not merely abstract concepts but are tangible assurances that sustain believers through the darkest times. These promises are likened to a fortress, providing protection and a sense of security amidst the storms of life. They are a testament to the unwavering commitment of a higher power to see us through every circumstance. The essence of these promises lies in their consistency and reliability; they do not waver with the changing tides of fortune but remain steadfast and true.

Furthermore, the promises that endure encourage a shift in perspective. They invite individuals to look beyond their immediate circumstances and to focus on the bigger picture. This shift in focus is crucial, as it transforms despair into hope and weakness into strength. By anchoring oneself in these promises of God which are relevant to believers, they are equipped to face any challenge with confidence, knowing that they are not alone. The assurance that these promises bring is a source of peace and comfort, allowing individuals to navigate life's trials with grace and dignity.

Moreover, these promises serve as a call to action. They inspire individuals to live with purpose, to strive for excellence, and to persevere despite setbacks. They remind us that every challenge is an opportunity for growth and that through faith, we can overcome any obstacle. The enduring nature of God's promises is a testament to their power and relevance in our lives. They are a constant reminder that no matter how difficult the journey may be, there is always hope and the possibility of triumph. You will win. The Bible says in Isaiah 41:10, "Do not fear, for I am with you; do not be discouraged, for I am your God. I will strengthen you; I will help you; I will uphold you with my righteous hand."

In essence, the promises that endure are more than mere words; they are a lifeline, a source of strength, and a testament to the enduring power of faith. They are a reminder that in the face of adversity, we are not alone and that with faith, all things are possible. As we hold onto these promises, we are empowered to break free from the cycle of defeat and to step into a life of victory and purpose.

Overcoming Doubt

In the face of life's challenges, doubt often emerges as a formidable adversary. Doubting God or His promises can erode trust, which is a fundamental aspect of faith.

The story in Genesis 3:1-4 depicts Satan, in the form of a serpent, questioning God's command to Adam and Eve, planting seeds of doubt about God's goodness and trustworthiness. The seed of doubt creeps into the mind, sowing seeds of uncertainty and hesitation that can stifle progress and undermine confidence, as Satan is still working in the same way. To overcome doubt, it is crucial to recognise it as a tool of Satan used to keep individuals trapped in a cycle of defeat. By understanding its nature and implementing strategies to counteract it, one can break free and move toward a life of victory. Doubt often arises from focusing too intently on circumstances, allowing them to overshadow one's faith and potential. It is essential to redirect focus from external situations to internal strength and faith. By taking eyes off the immediate challenges and placing trust in a higher purpose God has planned, one can begin to dismantle the power doubt holds over the mind. This shift in focus does not imply ignoring reality but rather acknowledging that circumstances are temporary and can be overcome with the right mindset. Another critical step in overcoming doubt is to actively resist the negative thoughts that accompany it, as to overcome doubt and negative thoughts, the Bible encourages actively resisting them and focusing on God's truth and promises. Verses like Philippians 4:8 and 2 Corinthians 10:5 emphasise replacing negative thoughts with positive, godly ones. These thoughts often manifest as fear, worry, and anxiety, which can paralyse decision-making and action. By consciously identifying and rejecting these thoughts, one can prevent them from taking root. It involves a deliberate choice to replace doubt with thoughts of hope and assurance stated in the relevant words of God to your situation, reinforcing the belief that one is capable of overcoming any obstacle. Faith plays a pivotal role in diminishing doubt. It acts as a counterbalance, providing the strength needed to face uncertainties with confidence. Cultivating faith involves nurturing a deep-seated belief in one's abilities and the assurance that support is available, whether through spiritual, emotional, or communal means. It requires an understanding that faith is not merely a passive state but an active choice to trust in positive outcomes despite current circumstances. In practical terms, overcoming doubt means taking actionable steps that align with one's goals and values. It involves setting clear intentions and pursuing them with determination, regardless of the doubts that may arise. By taking consistent actions, one can gradually erode the hold of doubt, replacing it with a sense of accomplishment and progress. Furthermore, surrounding oneself with a supportive community can provide encouragement and perspective, helping to reinforce confidence and diminish doubt. Engaging with others who share similar values and goals can create a network of support that fosters resilience and optimism.

In essence, overcoming doubt is about reclaiming power over one's thoughts and actions. It involves recognising doubt as a natural but conquerable challenge and employing strategies that reinforce faith, focus, and resilience. By doing so, individuals can break free from the cycle of defeat and move toward a life characterised by victory and fulfilment.

Living in Victory

Living a victorious life involves understanding that adversity is a part of the human experience, yet it need not define one's existence. Central to this understanding is the belief that ultimate victory is assured through divine provision and strength found in the Bible. Corinthians 15:57 says, "But thanks be to God, who gives us the victory through our Lord Jesus Christ." This perspective is rooted in the recognition that challenges are not arbitrary but a higher purpose in personal and spiritual development.

The first step to living in victory is just praying and acknowledging that every situation, no matter how daunting, is under divine control. This belief instills a sense of peace and assurance, knowing that circumstances are not beyond what one can bear. Philippians 4:6-7 also states, "Do not be anxious about anything, but in everything by prayer and supplication with thanksgiving let your requests be made known to God. And the peace of God, which surpasses all understanding, will guard your hearts and minds through Christ Jesus."

This conviction, based on the word of God, is supported by the idea that God limits the trials one faces, ensuring that they are within one's capacity to endure and overcome. This understanding transforms the perception of trials from obstacles to opportunities for growth and refinement.

Another crucial aspect of living victoriously is the ability to shift focus from the problem to the solution. This involves a conscious decision to fix one's eyes on the divine, relevant promises about your struggle rather than the immediate challenges. By doing so, one taps into a source of strength and wisdom that surpasses human understanding. This shift in focus is not a denial of reality but a strategic approach to engaging with it from a position of faith and confidence.

Moreover, living in victory requires active resistance against negative influences that seek to undermine faith and confidence in God for victory. This resistance is not passive but involves actively using spiritual resources such as prayer, meditation on words of God and the study of divine teachings of the Bible and proclaiming them with your mouth to fortify the mind and spirit. These practices serve as a reminder of the divine presence and support that is always available, reinforcing the belief that victory is not only possible but inevitable. The Bible portrays God as a "present help in trouble" in Psalm 46:1, stating, "God is our refuge and strength, a very present help in trouble."

An integral part of this victorious life is the cultivation of joy and gratitude, even in the midst of trials. The word of God says in 1 Thessalonians 5:18, "Give thanks in all circumstances, for this is God's will for you in Christ Jesus." Philippians 4:6: "Do not be anxious about anything, but in every situation, by prayer and petition, with thanksgiving, make your needs known to God."

This attitude of gratitude is not contingent on external circumstances but is a deliberate choice to acknowledge and appreciate the good that exists, even in difficult times, by putting your faith and trust in God. This practice of gratitude shifts the focus from lack to abundance, further empowering one to live in victory.

Finally, perseverance is key to maintaining a victorious stance. It involves steadfastness and resilience in the face of ongoing challenges, coupled with the unwavering belief that each step forward is a step closer to ultimate victory. Several Bible verses highlight the connection between perseverance, assurance, and divine grace, emphasising that faith-fuelled efforts are met with God's favour. Hebrews 11:1 states that "Now faith is the assurance of things hoped for, the conviction of things not seen.

This perseverance is fueled by the assurance that divine support is unwavering and that every effort made in faith is met with divine grace.

To live in victory, as a dynamic process of belief, focus, resistance, gratitude, and perseverance, is supported by biblical verses emphasising faith, endurance, and reliance on God, such as Romans 8:37, 1 Corinthians 15:57, and Philippians 4:13.

In conclusion, living in victory is a dynamic process that involves a continuous cycle of belief, focus, resistance, gratitude, and perseverance by contently trusting in the word of God in Hebrews 11:1, Philippians 4:6-7, James 1:12, Romans 15:13, and Joshua 1:9. It is a journey of transformation that transcends circumstances, enabling one to live a life marked by peace, joy, and triumph over adversity and sin.

4

Replacing Stress with Peace

The Gift of Peace

In the midst of life's challenges, a profound transformation can occur when one replaces stress with peace. This transformation is not merely a passive acceptance but an active choice to set one's mind on divine faithfulness, allowing a serene tranquillity to envelop the heart and mind. This is a peace that transcends understanding, a peace that is promised to those who trust in sovereign God, as articulated in Philippians 4:7, "And the peace of God, which surpasses all understanding, will guard your hearts and minds through Christ Jesus."

This verse speaks of a peace from God that is beyond human comprehension, a peace that will protect your emotions and thoughts. The assurance of everlasting strength as mentioned in the above words of God provides a foundation upon which one can stand firm, even when the storms of life threaten.

The meditation on sacred scripture encourages believers to find joy amidst trials, suggesting that these trials are not random acts of misfortune but opportunities for growth and spiritual participation in something greater. This perspective is highlighted through the exhortations of early apostles who urged followers to rejoice in their sufferings, not as a denial of their reality, but as a recognition of a deeper, transformative process at work. The Bible passages that speak to rejoicing in suffering, even in the face of hardship, include Romans 5:3-5, 1 Peter 4:12-13, and James 1:2-4, which emphasise that suffering can lead to endurance, character, and hope, and that sharing in Christ's sufferings is a cause for rejoicing.

Central to this transformation is the act of shifting focus from the overwhelming circumstances to the eternal truths found in spiritual teachings. This involves a deliberate decision to look beyond the immediate, often daunting, challenges and to fix one's gaze upon the enduring promises of divine presence and support. By doing so, believers can find themselves surrounded by a cloud of witnesses who have also navigated these paths, providing a source of encouragement and strength.

The spiritual journey is not without its battles. It requires resistance against the forces/devil that seek to instill fear and doubt. This resistance is not a passive stance but an active engagement through the word of God, as stated in James 4:7, "Submit yourselves, then, to God. Resist the devil, and he will flee from you," which clearly emphasising the importance of humility and spiritual resistance. utilising the above spiritual tools and armour provided for protection and empowerment. This involves casting out negative thoughts and binding the adversary's influence over one's circumstances, affirming the victory that has been promised. To combat negative thoughts and resist the adversary's influence, consider these Bible verses: 2 Corinthians 10:4-5 (taking every thought captive), 1 Peter 5:7-9 (casting your cares on God), and Ephesians 6:10-18 (spiritual warfare and the armour of God).

Faith plays a pivotal role in this process. It is not simply a belief but an active trust that manifests in action, as if the desired outcome has already been achieved. This faith, unwavering and steadfast, is essential for receiving the divine promises. Hebrews 10:23 says that "Let us hold fast the confession of our hope without wavering, for he who promised is faithful." It is a call to live in the assurance that what has been asked for in prayer has been granted, even before any tangible evidence is visible.

Ultimately, the path to peace is a journey of trust, a journey that requires letting go of control and placing it in the hands of the divine. It is a journey where one learns to replace every anxious thought with a prayer of thanksgiving, confident that every need will be met (Philippians 4:6-7). In this space, peace reigns, not because the circumstances have changed, but because the heart and mind are guarded by an unshakeable trust in the divine plan and God. This is the gift of peace, a profound and enduring presence that transforms the cycle of defeat into a cycle of victory.

Guarding the Mind

Satan's primary objective is to disrupt peace of mind by instilling worry, fear, and doubt, as mentioned in 2 Corinthians 11:3. "But I am afraid that just as Eve was deceived by the serpent's cunning, your minds may somehow be led astray from your sincere and pure devotion to Christ." These emotions in the heart are not just feelings; they are strategic assaults intended to keep individuals trapped in a cycle of defeat. When the mind is overwhelmed with worry, the ability to trust in God's promises diminishes, leaving one vulnerable to further attacks. The mind becomes a battlefield where every thought of fear and doubt must be actively resisted and cast out in the Name of Jesus.

Proverbs 4:23: Above all else, guard your heart, for everything you do flows from it. This verse emphasises the importance of protecting your thoughts and emotions, as they are the foundation of your actions and character. The first step in guarding the mind is recognising that worry is a tool used by Satan to choke the Word of God and render it ineffective in one's life. In describing the thorny ground, Matthew 13:22, Jesus says that "the worries of this life and the deceitfulness of wealth choke it [the Word], making it unfruitful." This recognition is crucial because worry can paralyse faith, making one double-minded and unstable in their ways. To counteract this, individuals are encouraged to take their eyes off their circumstances and fix them on Jesus and His Word, as mentioned in Proverbs 3:5-6: "Trust in the Lord with all your heart and lean not on your own understanding." This shift in focus is essential for releasing faith and receiving God's promises.

Another vital aspect of guarding the mind is the conscious decision to refuse the entry of fear and worry. This involves a proactive stance where one does not allow any thought that contradicts God's Word to take root. Instead, individuals are urged to cast all their anxieties on God, trusting that He cares and will provide as mentioned in 1 Peter 5:7, "Cast all your anxiety on him because he cares for you." This act of casting is not passive; it requires an active engagement of the will to throw one's concerns onto God, thereby allowing His peace to guard the heart and mind.

Furthermore, releasing faith is a critical component in this process. Faith is not just belief but an active trust in God's ability to fulfil His promises. By asking in faith without wavering, one aligns oneself with God's will, opening the door for His peace to cover their heart and mind. This peace is not dependent on circumstances but is a supernatural assurance that guards and protects against the assaults of fear and doubt.

In practical terms, guarding the mind also involves documenting and reflecting on moments when Satan attacks with fear, worry, and doubt. By identifying these instances, individuals can apply the cycle of victory, which includes taking eyes off circumstances (Hebrews 12:2 and Psalms 16:8), resisting Satan (James 4:7), refusing torment, and casting out negative thoughts (Philippians 4:8, 1 Corinthians 10:5, James 4:7, and 2 Corinthians 10:5). This strategic approach not only defends the mind but also empowers individuals to live in victory, free from the cycle of defeat.

Ultimately, guarding the mind requires vigilance and a steadfast commitment to God's Word by way of storing up God's Word as per Isaiah 26:3, which says, "You will keep him in perfect peace, whose mind is stayed on You, because he trusts in You." When you store up God's Word in your heart, the Spirit will remind you of it in your time of need and guard your mind. It is a continuous process of renewing the mind, resisting the enemy, and releasing faith in God's promises. Through this disciplined approach, individuals can break free from the cycle of defeat and live in the victory that God has intended.

Maintaining Focus on Jesus

In the midst of life's challenges, maintaining focus on Jesus is crucial for overcoming the cycle of defeat, as per Romans 8:37: "In all these things we are more than conquerors." The world around us is filled with distractions and troubles that can easily shift our gaze away from Jesus. We must consciously decide to turn our eyes away from the chaos of our circumstances and fix them on Jesus, the author and finisher of our faith (Hebrews 12:2). This act of focusing on Jesus is not a passive one; it requires active participation and a deliberate choice to trust in His promises and His sovereignty over our lives.

Please note that when we focus on our circumstances, we often find ourselves overwhelmed by fear, worry, and doubt. These emotions can cloud our judgement and paralyse our faith, making it difficult to see the path to victory that God has laid out for us. Instead of succumbing to these negative feelings, we are called to look to Jesus, who endured the cross and despised the shame for the joy set before Him. By considering His endurance and His triumph over sin and death, we can draw strength and encouragement to persevere through our trials.

The Bible reminds us that we are surrounded by a great cloud of witnesses (Hebrews 12:1), those who have gone before us and have lived lives of faith. Their examples serve as a testament to the power of keeping our eyes on Jesus. As we run the race set before us with patience, we lay aside every weight and the sin that so easily besets us. This requires a conscious effort to resist the distractions and temptations that seek to divert our attention from Christ.

Moreover, focusing on Jesus involves immersing ourselves in His Word, 1 Timotheus 4:15. The scriptures are a source of life and guidance, providing us with the wisdom and strength needed to navigate the complexities of life. By meditating on His Word day and night, we allow His truths to penetrate our hearts and minds, equipping us to stand firm against the schemes of the enemy.

In practical terms, maintaining focus on Jesus means prioritising our relationship with Him above all else. It involves setting aside time for prayer, worship, and studying the Bible, even when life's demands seem overwhelming. It means trusting Him with our burdens and casting all our cares upon Him, knowing that He cares for us and is faithful to sustain us. As we fix our eyes on Jesus, we begin to see our circumstances in a new light. What once seemed insurmountable becomes an opportunity for God to demonstrate His power and faithfulness. Our perspective shifts from one of defeat to one of victory as we realise that nothing is impossible for those who believe. In this way, by keeping our focus on Jesus, we break free from the cycle of defeat and step into the abundant life He has promised.

Walking in Tranquillity

In the midst of life's turmoil, finding a path to peace is crucial. The concept of walking in tranquillity involves a deliberate shift of focus from the chaos surrounding us to the inner peace promised by faith. This tranquillity is not a passive state but an active pursuit of peace that guards the heart and mind against the storms of life. Romans 5:1 says, "Therefore, since we have been justified by faith, we have peace with God through our Lord Jesus Christ."

To begin this journey, it is essential to replace stress with peace. This involves a conscious decision to set our minds on faithfulness and promises of God rather than on the immediate challenges we face. By doing so, we allow a sense of calm to permeate our thoughts, much like a gentle breeze that soothes the soul amidst a tempest. The peace we seek is not an absence of challenges but a state of assurance in the midst of them.

Another important aspect is the practice of rejoicing even in trials. This might seem counterintuitive, but it is a powerful strategy for maintaining tranquillity. Rejoicing shifts the focus from the problem to the potential for growth and the hidden blessings within each trial. To shift focus from problems and cultivate joy, consider Philippians 4:4: "Rejoice in the Lord always; again, I will say, rejoice." This verse encourages a constant state of joy rooted in God, regardless of circumstances. It transforms our perspective and strengthens our resolve, allowing us to face difficulties with a positive mindset.

Moreover, taking one's eyes off the immediate circumstances and fixing them on higher purposes for your life (Jeremiah 29:11) can profoundly impact one's peace of mind. This does not mean ignoring the reality of our situations but rather viewing them through a lens of faith and hope in God and His word. By focusing on enduring values and promises of the word of God, we find strength and peace that surpasses understanding.

Resisting negative influences and thoughts is also vital. In the journey towards tranquillity, one must be vigilant against the forces and powers of darkness the devil uses that seek to disrupt peace. This involves a proactive stance, using spiritual and mental tools to safeguard one's peace. In 1 Peter 5:8-9, we are urged to exercise self-control and vigilance in our lives as followers of Jesus Christ. The verse portrays our adversary, the devil, as a prowling, roaring lion, constantly seeking opportunities to devour and undermine our faith. By resisting these influences by the word of God, we maintain control over our thoughts and emotions, ensuring they align with our pursuit of tranquillity.

Releasing faith is another cornerstone of walking in tranquillity. This involves trusting in the promises of provision and care available in the word of God, knowing that our needs will be met. It is a surrender to the belief that there is a greater plan at work, one that is for our ultimate good (Jeremiah 29:11). This trust is not blind but informed by past experiences and the assurance of a faithful journey.

Finally, perseverance in this journey is key. The road to tranquillity is not without its obstacles, but with perseverance, each step becomes a testament to the strength and resilience fostered by peace. In this way, tranquillity becomes both the journey and the destination, a continuous cycle of renewal and strength.

5

Resisting the Enemy

Identifying the Attack

In the realm of spiritual battles, identifying the nature and source of the attack is crucial to breaking free from cycles of defeat. Identify what is defeating you or overcoming you. What kind of thing is defeating you? The adversary often exploits everyday circumstances, weaving them into a web of confusion, doubt, and fear. This strategy is designed to distract and destabilise individuals, preventing them from realising their potential and achieving victory through faith. Recognising these tactics is the first step towards overcoming them.

The adversary's primary aim is to manipulate circumstances to create a sense of helplessness and defeat. By focusing on the immediate challenges—be it financial difficulties, health issues, or relational conflicts—individuals often overlook the broader spiritual implications of these situations. The key to countering these attacks lies in shifting focus from the problem to the solution, which is found in spiritual resilience and divine promises.

Fear and doubt are potent tools used to cloud judgement and paralyse action. When faced with daunting circumstances, the natural reaction is to succumb to fear, allowing it to overshadow faith. However, it is in these moments that faith must be exercised the most. The strength to overcome adversity does not come from the absence of challenges but from the ability to trust in God & His word despite them. This trust is what breaks the cycle of fear and inaugurates a cycle of victory. We must understand that fear is a spirit, as mentioned in 2 Timothy 1:7. "For God hath not given us the spirit of fear but of power and of love and of a sound mind." Moreover, it is essential to understand that the adversary's attacks are not merely random acts of aggression but are often calculated moves aimed at exploiting specific weaknesses. Biblical Verses Supporting the View in 1 Peter 5:8: "Be alert and of sound mind, because your enemy the devil is prowling around like a hungry lion, looking for someone to devour." Ephesians 6:12: "For our struggle is not against enemies of flesh and blood, but against the rulers, against the authorities, against the powers of this dark world and against the spiritual forces of evil in the heavenly realms." 2 Corinthians 2:11: "We do not want you to be ignorant of the devil's schemes."

By identifying the patterns, individuals can better prepare themselves to resist and ultimately overcome. This involves a proactive approach to spiritual growth, where one actively seeks to fortify their mind against doubt and fear through meditation on spiritual truths and promises.

Another aspect of identifying the attack involves recognising the internal dialogues that occur during these challenging times. The adversary often plants seeds of doubt and discouragement, which, if left unchecked, can grow into overwhelming obstacles. It is crucial to counter these negative thoughts with affirmations of faith and declarations of divine truth of the word of God. By doing so, one not only resists the attack but also strengthens their spiritual foundation.

In conclusion, identifying the attack requires a combination of awareness, spiritual discernment, and proactive faith. It involves acknowledging the reality of the situation without allowing it to dictate one's response. Instead, individuals are encouraged to rely on their spiritual resources, drawing strength from their faith and the promises that come with it in the word of God. Through this process, the cycle of defeat is broken, and a new cycle of victory begins, characterised by resilience, hope, and unwavering trust in God and His loving word.

Arming with God's Armour

In the spiritual battle against the forces of darkness, believers are called to equip themselves with the armour of God. The word of God says "put on the whole armour of God", which comes from Ephesians 6:11-18, urging believers to be prepared for spiritual warfare by equipping themselves with God's protection and strength. These divine armours are not just a metaphorical concept but a powerful reality that enables Christians to stand firm against the adversities and schemes of Satan. This armour includes various elements, each serving a specific purpose in protecting and empowering the believer.

The first component is the belt of truth, which symbolises the importance of honesty and integrity. Truth acts as a stabilising force, holding together the other pieces of the armour and providing a foundation for righteous living. Without truth, a believer's spiritual armour would fall apart, leaving them vulnerable to deception and falsehoods.

Next is the breastplate of righteousness, which guards the heart and vital organs against spiritual attacks. Righteousness, in this context, refers to living in accordance with God's standards and being in right standing with Him. It is a protective barrier against the accusations and guilt that the enemy tries to impose.

The footwear of the gospel of peace emphasises readiness and stability. Just as soldiers need sturdy shoes to march into battle, believers require the assurance and peace that come from the gospel. This peace enables them to stand firm and move forward, even in the face of conflict and trials.

The shield of faith is crucial for extinguishing the fiery darts of doubt, fear, and temptation launched by the enemy. Faith acts as a defensive weapon, absorbing and neutralising these attacks. It requires active trust in God's promises and His character, providing confidence that He will fulfil His word regardless of the circumstances.

The helmet of salvation protects the mind, which is often the battlefield where spiritual warfare is most intense. Salvation assures the believer of their identity in Christ and their eternal security, fortifying their mind against the lies and discouragements of Satan.

Lastly, the sword of the Spirit, which is the word of God, is the only offensive weapon in the armour. It represents the power of Scripture to cut through the enemy's deceptions and bring truth to light. By wielding the sword effectively, believers can counteract the enemy's attacks and advance in spiritual maturity.

Prayer is the final element that binds the armour together, empowering each piece with divine strength and guidance. Through prayer, believers maintain constant communication with God, ensuring they remain vigilant and prepared for the spiritual battles they face.

By understanding and utilising the full armour of God, Christians can break free from the cycle of defeat and live victoriously. It requires not only wearing the armour but also actively engaging in the spiritual disciplines that strengthen each component. In doing so, believers can withstand any challenge and emerge triumphant, secure in the knowledge that God fights for them and with them.

The Battle of the Mind

In the realm of spiritual warfare, the mind is often the primary battlefield. The adversary, through subtle tactics, seeks to infiltrate and dominate this personal territory. One of the most pervasive strategies employed is the introduction of worry. This emotion, seemingly harmless, can paralyse faith and render the word of God ineffective in one's life. Worry acts as a chokehold, suffocating the seeds of faith before they have the opportunity to take root and flourish. It is imperative to recognise that worry is not merely a human condition but a deliberate strategy of the adversary to keep individuals trapped in a cycle of defeat.

The process begins subtly, whatever the circumstances are or else we are facing. Circumstances arise that appear overwhelming, and the natural reaction is to dwell on these issues, to fixate on potential outcomes. This fixation gives rise to fear and doubt, emotions that directly oppose the tenets of faith. As the mind becomes consumed with these negative thoughts, the ability to trust in divine promises diminishes. The adversary knows that a mind preoccupied with worry is a mind that is not focused on faith. Without faith, the power of the word of God is diminished, and the cycle of defeat perpetuates.

To combat this, one must actively resist the intrusion of worry. This is not a passive endeavour but a conscious decision to redirect one's focus. Instead of fixating on the problem, one must fix their eyes on the solution—faith in divine providence. This requires a deliberate act of will, a choice to cast all anxieties upon a God as mentioned in the Bible. In doing so, peace, which surpasses all understanding, is invoked, guarding both heart and mind against further assault (Philippians 4:7).

Moreover, the battle of the mind is not fought in isolation. It requires the reinforcement of spiritual practices such as prayer, meditation on scripture/word of God, and a community of reliable support of a mature believer/elder/Pastor. These elements serve as fortifications, strengthening the resolve and providing the necessary tools to withstand the adversary's attacks. By immersing oneself in these practices, the seeds of faith are nurtured and given the opportunity to grow, ultimately breaking the cycle of defeat.

The adversary's goal is not just to disrupt momentarily but to establish a stronghold that keeps individuals in perpetual defeat. However, by recognising worry as a strategic tool of the enemy, individuals can take proactive steps to dismantle this stronghold. It involves a transformation of the mind, a renewal that aligns thoughts with faith rather than fear. This transformation is not instantaneous but requires persistence and dedication.

In essence, the battle of the mind is a journey towards victory. It is about reclaiming the territory that rightfully belongs to the individual/ours and refusing to allow the adversary to plant seeds of doubt and fear. Through vigilance and faith, the cycle of defeat can be broken, and a new cycle of victory established. This victory is not only personal but extends to all facets of life, influencing relationships, work, and spiritual growth. The mind, once a battlefield, becomes a fortress of peace, fortified by faith and impervious to the adversary's tactics.

Victory Through Resistance

In the face of challenging circumstances, resistance becomes a pivotal strategy for achieving victory. It is crucial to understand that while adversities may appear overwhelming, they serve as opportunities for growth and triumph. This perspective shift is essential in breaking the cycle of defeat that often ensnares individuals.

The adversary's/devil's primary tactic is to exploit circumstances to instill fear and doubt, thereby weakening resolve. Several Bible verses highlight the devil's tactics of exploiting circumstances to instill fear and doubt, ultimately aiming to weaken resolve, including 1 Peter 5:8-9, Ephesians 6:11-12, and James 4:7-8. However, recognising this strategy allows one to resist effectively. The first step in this resistance is to acknowledge that every trial presents a provision for victory. This mindset empowers individuals to confront challenges not with despair but with confidence in eventual triumph.

Arming oneself with spiritual tools is vital in this struggle. The armour of faith, as described in spiritual texts, provides protection and strength. It is not enough to passively hope for change; active engagement in resisting negative influences is required. This involves a conscious effort to cast out fear and doubt, replacing them with faith and assurance in relevant divine promises of the word of God.

Moreover, maintaining focus on positive outcomes rather than current difficulties is necessary. Circumstances are transient, but the lessons and strength gained from enduring them are lasting. By fixing attention on these enduring truths, individuals can navigate through temporary setbacks without losing sight of their ultimate goals.

Prayer and meditation play significant roles in fortifying the mind against defeatist thoughts. Through these practices and putting faith in divine relevant promises in the word of God, individuals can access peace and clarity, which are essential in maintaining a resilient spirit. These moments of reflection provide the strength needed to continue resisting adverse circumstances.

Furthermore, community support and shared experiences offer additional strength. Engaging with others who are reliable in Christ and who face similar challenges fosters a sense of solidarity and shared purpose, reinforcing the determination to resist defeat.

In summary, victory through resistance is not merely about enduring hardships but transforming them into stepping stones toward success. By utilising spiritual resources available in the word of God, maintaining a positive focus, and engaging in supportive communities, i.e., relevant brethren in Christ, individuals can effectively break free from cycles of defeat and enter a realm of sustained victory. The journey requires perseverance and faith, but the promise of transformation and growth makes it a worthy pursuit. Each act of resistance strengthens the resolve, bringing one closer to a life defined not by defeat but by continuous victory.

6

Enduring Through Trials

The Purpose of Trials

Trials are an integral part of the human experience, and understanding their purpose can transform how one navigates through life's challenges. When facing trials, the Bible encourages perseverance and faith, reminding us that these challenges can strengthen our character and bring us closer to God. Here are some key verses about trials: James 1:2-4, Romans 12:12, and John 16:33. Trials are not random occurrences but are permitted by a God to achieve a greater good. They serve to refine, mature, and strengthen individuals, fostering endurance and resilience in the face of adversity. This perspective aligns with the idea that trials are designed to perfect and complete individuals, ensuring they lack nothing essential for personal growth.

One key aspect of trials is the belief that they are under divine control, with limitations placed on them. This means that no trial or circumstance can overwhelm an individual beyond their capacity to endure. This assurance provides comfort and courage, knowing that every challenge is accompanied by the strength to overcome it, as mentioned in 1 Corinthians 10:13. This controlled aspect of trials underscores the idea that they serve a beneficial purpose, intended to build character and fortitude.

Furthermore, trials are seen as opportunities for spiritual and personal development. They encourage individuals to rely on faith and divine promises of God, reinforcing trust in Him. This reliance fosters a deeper connection with God and cultivates a sense of peace amidst turmoil. The process of enduring trials is likened to the refining of gold, where impurities are removed, leaving a stronger and more resilient core.

In addition to personal growth, trials are believed to have a communal benefit. They provide opportunities to inspire and uplift others who may be facing similar challenges. By overcoming trials, individuals can become beacons of hope and examples of perseverance for their communities, demonstrating that victory is possible despite adversity.

Moreover, trials are perceived as a test of faith, prompting individuals to exercise their spiritual muscles and develop a robust faith that can withstand life's storms. This testing of faith is not intended to break individuals but to empower them, equipping them with the necessary tools to navigate future challenges with confidence and strength.

In essence, the purpose of trials is multifaceted, serving both individual and collective purposes. They are not merely obstacles but are transformative experiences that lead to personal and spiritual enrichment. By understanding the purpose of trials, individuals can embrace them as opportunities for growth and development, ultimately leading to a more fulfilled and victorious life. Let us see the Bible verses mention the same; read these promises, believe them and walk in victory over trials.

James 1:2-4: "Consider it pure joy, my brothers and sisters, whenever you face trials of many kinds, because you know that the testing of your faith produces perseverance. Let perseverance finish its work so that you may be mature and complete, not lacking anything."

1 Peter 1:6-7: In this you rejoice, though now for a little while, if necessary, you have been grieved by various trials so that the tested genuineness of your faith—more precious than gold that perishes though it is tested by fire—may be found to result in praise and glory and honour at the revelation of Jesus Christ."

Romans 5:3-5: "We also glory in our sufferings, because we know that suffering produces perseverance; perseverance, character; and character, hope. And hope does not disappoint us, because God's love has been poured out into our hearts through the Holy Spirit, whom he has given to us."

Our Lord Jesus also faced and overcame them. Jesus said in John 16:33, I have told you all this so that you may have peace in me. Here on earth, you will have many trials and sorrows. But take heart; I have overcome the world."

Building Endurance

In the pursuit of overcoming defeat, the development of endurance is crucial. Endurance is not merely the ability to withstand adversity but is a transformative process that strengthens character and faith. This process often begins with a shift in perspective, recognising that challenges are not permanent obstacles but opportunities for growth and refinement. The trials one faces are not designed to break them but to build resilience and fortitude, enabling them to emerge stronger and more determined. Let us see, 1 Peter 5:10: "And the God of all grace, who called you to his eternal glory in Christ, after you have suffered a little while, will himself restore you and make you strong, firm and steadfast." This verse promises that after suffering, God will restore and strengthen believers, making them firm and steadfast.

One of the foundational aspects of building endurance is understanding the role of circumstances in personal development. Circumstances, often orchestrated by forces beyond one's control, can seem overwhelming. However, it is crucial to acknowledge that these situations are not without purpose. They serve as the crucible through which endurance is forged. By embracing this viewpoint, individuals can transform their approach to adversity, viewing it as a necessary step in their journey toward greater strength and maturity.

A key element in developing endurance is maintaining a focus on long-term goals rather than immediate discomfort. This focus helps to cultivate patience and perseverance, essential traits for anyone striving to break cycles of defeat. Patience allows individuals to endure temporary setbacks with grace, knowing that each challenge is a stepping stone toward eventual success. Perseverance, meanwhile, fuels the continuous effort required to overcome obstacles, no matter how daunting they may appear.

Furthermore, building endurance involves nurturing a mindset that rejects defeatism. This mindset is characterised by a refusal to succumb to discouragement, instead opting for a proactive approach to problem-solving. By actively seeking solutions through the word of God and remaining committed to personal growth, individuals can effectively counteract the negative impact of adverse circumstances. This resilience is not innate but is cultivated through consistent practice and a willingness to learn from each experience.

In addition, the support of a community or network can significantly enhance one's ability to build endurance. Sharing experiences and receiving encouragement from others who have faced similar challenges can provide the necessary motivation to continue pushing forward. This communal aspect of endurance building highlights the importance of connection and solidarity in overcoming defeat.

Finally, it is essential to recognise that building endurance is a continuous process. It requires ongoing effort and a commitment to self-improvement. Each victory, no matter how small, contributes to a cumulative sense of strength and capability, reinforcing the belief that one can overcome any obstacle. By approaching life with a mindset focused on growth and resilience, individuals can transform the cycle of defeat into a cycle of victory, paving the way for lasting success and fulfilment.

Strength in Weakness

In the realm of spiritual growth, paradoxes abound, and one of the most profound is the concept of strength emerging from weakness. Isaiah 40:29-31 promises, "He gives power to the weak and strength to the powerless," emphasising that God empowers those who are physically or emotionally weak. This principle is deeply embedded in the spiritual journey, where individuals often find their greatest empowerment not in moments of triumph but in those of vulnerability and trial. The notion that divine strength is perfected in human weakness is a recurring theme that challenges conventional understandings of power and resilience.

The Apostle Paul offers a compelling narrative that illustrates this paradox. He speaks of a 'thorn in the flesh' (2 Corinthians 12:7), a persistent affliction (messenger of Satan) that he pleaded with God to remove. Instead of granting relief, God provided a profound revelation: 'My grace is sufficient for you (2 Corinthians 12:9), for my power is made perfect in weakness.' This response highlights a divine strategy that transforms personal limitations into avenues for spiritual empowerment. In accepting his vulnerabilities, Paul discovered that his weaknesses became the very channels through which God's power was most effectively manifested. This idea is rooted in the Bible, particularly in 2 Corinthians 12:9-10, where Paul states, "My grace is sufficient for you, for my power is made perfect in weakness. Therefore, I will boast all the more willingly of my weaknesses, that the power of Christ may rest upon me. For the sake of Christ, I am content with weaknesses, insults, hardships, persecutions, and calamities; for when I am weak, then I am strong."

This transformative process involves a shift in perspective. It requires individuals to relinquish the illusion of self-sufficiency and embrace a posture of dependence on God and His relevant words. This surrender is not synonymous with defeat; rather, it is an acknowledgement of the limitations inherent in human strength and the boundless potential of divine intervention. Through this lens, weaknesses are not seen as liabilities but as opportunities for divine strength to be displayed.

The story of Job further exemplifies this principle. Despite enduring unimaginable suffering and loss, Job's faith remained unshaken. His journey was marked by moments of profound despair, yet it culminated in a deeper understanding of divine sovereignty and goodness. Job's restoration, which included receiving twice as much as he had before his trials, underscores the potential for renewal and blessing that can emerge from periods of weakness and suffering.

In practical terms, embracing weakness involves cultivating resilience through faith in God and His word. It is about finding peace amidst turmoil, joy in trials, and strength in the acknowledgement of human frailty. This inner resilience is not a denial of reality but a profound trust in the divine purpose that transcends immediate circumstances. It encourages individuals to look beyond their limitations and to see their trials as integral to their spiritual development and ultimate victory.

The path to strength through weakness is not devoid of struggle. It demands perseverance, a steadfast commitment to faith, and an openness to divine guidance through the word of God. It is through these trials that character is refined and spiritual maturity is achieved. By embracing their weaknesses, individuals can find themselves aligned with a deeper, more enduring source (word of God) of strength that empowers them to overcome the cycles of defeat and step into a life marked by divine victory.

Ultimately, the strength found in weakness is a testament to the transformative power of faith. It affirms the belief that in the face of adversity, there is an opportunity for growth and a promise of divine strength through the word of God that equips individuals to rise above their circumstances and live victoriously.

Perseverance Pays Off

In the realm of spiritual resilience, perseverance emerges as a fundamental principle that underpins the journey from defeat to victory. It is not merely about enduring hardship but about maintaining faith and steadfastness in the face of adversity. This unwavering commitment is essential for breaking the cycle of defeat that often ensnares the faithful.

The concept of perseverance is deeply rooted in the understanding that trials and tribulations are not obstacles to be feared but opportunities for growth and spiritual fortification. This perspective shifts the focus from the immediate discomfort of the trials to the long-term benefits of enduring them with faith. It is about recognizing that each challenge is a stepping stone towards a greater purpose, one that is orchestrated by a higher power with the ultimate goal of nurturing spiritual maturity and resilience.

In the face of adversity, the faithful are called to persist in their spiritual practices, such as prayer and meditation on the word of God, which serve as anchors during tumultuous times. These practices are not merely rituals; they are lifelines that connect the individual to a source of divine strength and wisdom. Through prayer, individuals can release their burdens and anxieties, entrusting them to a higher power that promises to provide strength and guidance.

Moreover, perseverance is about maintaining a positive outlook even when circumstances seem dire. It involves cultivating an attitude of gratitude and hope, which acts as a shield against the corrosive effects of doubt and despair. This mindset is not about ignoring the reality of the situation but about choosing to focus on the potential for divine intervention and the eventual triumph over adversity.

The path of perseverance requires the faithful to remain vigilant against the subtle strategies of the devil to defeat, such as fear and doubt, which can undermine their resolve. By continually affirming their faith and trust in the word of God, individuals can resist these negative influences and maintain their spiritual equilibrium. This resistance is not a passive act but an active engagement in spiritual warfare, where the individual uses their faith as a weapon against the forces of defeat.

Ultimately, as James 1:12 states, "Blessed is the one who perseveres under trial, because when that person has stood the test, they will receive the crown of life that the Lord has promised to those who love him." So, perseverance is rewarded with the crown of life, a metaphorical representation of the spiritual rewards that await those who remain steadfast in their faith. This promise serves as a powerful motivator, encouraging individuals to persist in their journey despite the challenges they may face. It is a reminder that the trials of today are temporary and that the rewards of perseverance are eternal.

In conclusion, perseverance is a vital component in breaking the cycle of defeat, as mentioned in the following Bible verses that emphasise that perseverance is crucial in overcoming adversity and breaking cycles of defeat, offering hope and strength through trials, as seen in verses like James 1:12 and Hebrews 12:1. It empowers individuals to face their circumstances with courage and faith, knowing that they are not alone in their struggles. By embracing perseverance, the faithful can transform their trials into triumphs and emerge stronger and more resilient in their spiritual journey.

7

Harnessing Divine Strength

Recognising God's Power

Understanding the magnitude of divine power involves acknowledging the omnipotence that governs the universe. This understanding begins with the realisation that God's power is not only limitless but also ever-present in our lives. Several Bible verses emphasise God's unlimited and ever-present power. Bible verses highlight his power in creation, sustaining the universe, and acting in the lives of believers. For example, Colossians 1:16 states that all things were created through and for God. Similarly, Hebrews 1:3 describes him as upholding the universe by the word of his power. Additionally, Ephesians 3:20 emphasises that God is able to do immeasurably more than we can ask or imagine. It manifests in various forms, guiding, protecting, and providing for us in ways we might not always recognise. The essence of recognising God's power lies in appreciating the subtle and overt ways it influences our daily existence.

One of the fundamental aspects of divine power is its role in creation. Everything that exists, from the vastness of the cosmos to the intricacies of human life, is a testament to this power. The intricate balance of nature, the laws of physics, and the complexity of life forms all reflect a power beyond human comprehension. This power is not just about creation but also about sustaining life, ensuring that everything functions in harmony. Colossians 1:16 states that "in him all things were created: things in heaven and on earth, visible and invisible, whether thrones or powers or rulers or authorities; all things have been created through him and for him." Recognising this aspect of God's power can lead to a deeper appreciation for the world around us and our place within it.

Moreover, God's power is evident in the moral and spiritual laws that govern human existence. Romans 1:18-20:

"For the wrath of God is revealed from heaven against all ungodliness and injustice of those who by their injustice suppress the truth... For since the creation of the world, God's invisible qualities—his eternal power and divine nature—have been clearly seen, being understood through what he has made, so that people are without excuse." This passage speaks to God's power being revealed through creation and the moral law inscribed in human hearts, demonstrating that humans have a natural awareness of God's standards. These biblical laws offer guidance and support, helping individuals navigate the challenges of life. They provide a framework for living a life that is aligned with the divine will of God as per the Bible, promoting peace, justice, and compassion. Understanding this power, which comes from the word of God when we obey them, involves acknowledging the importance of these laws and their role in shaping our actions and decisions. It is through these spiritual principles that individuals can find strength and resilience, even in the face of adversity and the devil.

In addition to creation and moral guidance, divine power is also about transformation. It has the ability to change hearts and minds, leading to personal growth and spiritual development. This transformative power is evident in the lives of those who have overcome significant challenges by obeying the living word of God, finding strength and hope through their faith in it. It is a power of the word of God that can heal wounds, restore relationships, and bring about profound change in individuals and communities. Recognising this aspect of God's power involves being open to change and willing to embrace the potential for growth.

Furthermore, God's power is a source of comfort and reassurance. Isaiah 41:10, for example, assures, "Fear not, for I am with you; be not dismayed, for I am your God; I will strengthen you; I will help you; I will uphold you with my righteous right hand." Psalm 46:1 also declares, "God is our refuge and strength, an ever-present help in trouble. In times of trouble or uncertainty, it provides a sense of peace and security, reminding us that we are not alone and He is with us. This power is a constant presence, offering support and guidance when we need it most. It is a reminder that, regardless of the circumstances, there is a greater force at work, orchestrating events for our ultimate good.

Recognising this power involves trusting in God's plan, even when it is not immediately apparent.

Ultimately, recognising God's power is about seeing the divine in every aspect of life. It is about acknowledging the presence of a higher power that is actively involved in the world, guiding and shaping our experiences. This recognition can lead to a deeper sense of purpose and meaning, inspiring individuals to live in accordance with divine principles. It is a journey of faith and understanding, one that enriches the soul and brings us closer to the divine.

Relying on God's Might

In the face of life's trials and tribulations, it is essential to recognise the might and supremacy of God. Often, circumstances arise that seem insurmountable, and the adversary, the devil, uses these moments to instil doubt and fear. However, the key to overcoming these challenges lies in understanding that God is in control and His power is accessible to us, as Philippians 4:13 says ("I can do all things through Christ who strengthens me"). Our reliance on God's might is not a passive act but an active engagement with His promises and strength available in the Bible.

The Bible provides numerous examples of individuals who faced overwhelming odds yet emerged victorious by depending on God. Job, for instance, endured severe trials, losing his possessions, health, and family. Despite the intense suffering and the temptation to succumb to despair, Job's story illustrates the resilience and ultimate redemption that comes from trusting in God's purpose. His trials were not without reason; they refined his faith, and in the end, God restored him abundantly, as described in Job 42:10-17, how God restored Job's losses, even giving him more than he had before.

Similarly, the Apostle Paul faced numerous hardships, including persecution and imprisonment, as stated in 2 Corinthians 11:23-28, where he recounts being imprisoned, beaten, and even near death multiple times. Yet, he remained steadfast, recognising that his strength came from God. Paul understood that in his weakness, God's power was made perfect, as mentioned by him in 2 Corinthians 12:9-10. Paul states, "But he said to me, 'My grace is sufficient for you, for my power is made perfect in weakness. This acknowledgement allowed him to persevere through adversity, knowing that each challenge was an opportunity for God's might to manifest.

God's might is not just about delivering us from difficult circumstances but also about transforming us through them. Each trial is a chance to deepen our faith and grow spiritually. God provides the strength needed to endure and overcome, turning what the enemy intends for harm into a testimony of victory. By relying on God's might, we align ourselves with His divine purpose and plan, which is always for our good. In James, James conveys in chapter 1:2-4: "Consider it a great joy, my brothers and sisters, whenever you experience various trials, because you know that the testing of your faith produces endurance. And endurance produces character, and character produces hope. And that hope will not disappoint you."

The process of relying on God requires us to shift our focus from the problems we face to the greatness of God. This shift in perspective is crucial because it enables us to see beyond the immediate challenges to the victory that God has promised. It involves a conscious decision to trust in His sovereignty and faithfulness, even when the situation seems dire.

Moreover, engaging with God's might involves utilising the spiritual resources He has provided. Prayer, the Word of God, and the fellowship of believers are vital tools in our spiritual arsenal. The word of God says in Hebrews 10:25, part of the New Testament, encourages believers to "not forsake the assembling of ourselves together, as is the manner of some" and instead to "exhort one another". It stresses the importance of regular Christian fellowship, emphasising that it's not just a tradition but a vital practice for encouragement and spiritual growth, especially as the return of Christ draws near. Through prayer, we communicate with God, expressing our dependence on Him and seeking His guidance and strength. The Bible serves as a source of encouragement and wisdom, reminding us of God's promises and past faithfulness. Fellowship with other believers provides support and accountability, helping us to remain steadfast in our faith.

Ultimately, relying on God's might is about living in a state of continuous trust and obedience. It is about acknowledging that while we may not have control over our circumstances, we serve a God who does. He is omnipotent, and His love for us is unfailing. By placing our trust in Him, we can face any challenge with confidence, knowing that He is working all things together for our good (Romans 8:28). This reliance is not a one-time act but a daily commitment to walk by faith, assured that God's might is sufficient for every need.

Empowered by the Spirit

In the Christian life, there is a profound source of strength and victory that believers can tap into, which is the empowerment of the Holy Spirit. This empowerment is not just a theological concept but a practical reality that enables individuals to overcome the challenges and trials they face. The Holy Spirit is a vital presence in the life of a believer, providing guidance, comfort, and power to live a victorious Christian life.

The role of the Holy Spirit is multifaceted, acting as a guide, a comforter, and a source of strength. Several Bible verses emphasise the Holy Spirit's role as a personal guide and helper for believers. Verses like John 14:26 and Romans 8:26 highlight the Spirit's teaching, guidance, and intercession, demonstrating its active presence in our lives. This divine empowerment allows believers to transcend their natural limitations and operate in a realm of spiritual authority. The Spirit empowers believers to resist the strategies of Satan, who seeks to keep them in a cycle of defeat through stress, fear, and doubt. The Holy Spirit empowers believers to resist Satan's strategies by providing discernment, strength, and understanding of his tactics. By being led by the Spirit, believers can recognise lies and temptations, stand firm in faith, and resist spiritual attacks.

The Spirit strengthens believers to overcome and resist the devil's schemes. By relying on the Holy Spirit, believers can break free from these cycles and enter into a life of victory.

One of the key aspects of being empowered by the Spirit is the ability to experience peace in the midst of turmoil (Philippians 4:4-6). This peace, which surpasses all understanding, guards the hearts and minds of believers, enabling them to remain steadfast even when circumstances are unfavourable. The peace of the Holy Spirit is not dependent on external conditions but is a deep-seated assurance that God is in control and is working all things together for good.

Additionally, the Holy Spirit provides believers with the strength to persevere. When faced with trials, it is easy to become weary and lose heart. However, the Spirit renews the strength of believers, allowing them to press on and remain faithful. This perseverance is crucial in breaking the cycle of defeat and achieving victory in every area of life.

Moreover, the Holy Spirit empowers believers to live a life of faith. This faith is not merely intellectual assent but a dynamic trust in God's promises. The Holy Spirit enables believers to see beyond their circumstances and trust in God's unchanging nature. As believers exercise their faith, they find that God is faithful to deliver them and to fulfil His promises, no matter how daunting the situation may seem. 2 Corinthians 1:20 conveys that "For no matter how many promises God has made, they are 'Yes' in Christ. And so, through him, the 'Amen' is spoken by us to the glory of God."

The empowerment by the Holy Spirit also involves a transformation of perspective. Believers are encouraged to fix their eyes not on their problems but on God, who is greater than any challenge they might face. 1 John 4:4 says that "You, dear children, are from God and have overcome them, because the one who is in you is greater than the one who is in the world." This shift in focus is essential in overcoming the enemy's attempts to keep believers bound in defeat.

In conclusion, being empowered by the Spirit is a crucial aspect of breaking the whatever cycle of defeat that one is facing. It involves living in the reality of God's presence and power, experiencing His peace, persevering through trials, exercising faith, and maintaining a God-centred perspective. This empowerment is available to every believer, enabling them to live in victory over the challenges of life. By embracing the Holy Spirit's empowerment, believers can rise above any circumstances and walk in the fullness of God's promises.

Living Beyond Limits

Breaking free from the confines of a limiting mindset requires a steadfast commitment to transcending the barriers that often hold us back. The essence of living beyond limits is rooted in the understanding that obstacles are not permanent fixtures but rather temporary challenges that can be overcome with the right mindset and tools. To navigate through these challenges, one must first recognise the power of perspective. By shifting focus from the obstacles to the possibilities & walking from defeat to victory, individuals can harness a mindset that propels them beyond their current limitations. The devil wants us to trust in defeat, facing a cycle of defeat again and again with no hope for victory, but the word of God says we can do all things through Christ (Philippians 4:13). Hence, the word of God in Philippians 4:13, "I can do all this through him who gives me strength," encourages us to focus on the unlimited power of God and not on self-defeat.

A critical component in this journey is the cultivation of resilience. Resilience is not merely the ability to withstand adversity but the capacity to adapt and grow in the face of challenges. It involves developing a mental framework that views setbacks as opportunities for growth and learning. This perspective shift is essential for breaking the cycle of defeat and moving towards a cycle of victory. Embracing resilience means acknowledging the inevitability of challenges while maintaining a focus on the potential for positive outcomes by putting trust in the word of God.

Moreover, living beyond limits involves a proactive approach to personal development. It requires individuals to continuously seek Bible knowledge and skills available through the word of God that enable them to navigate their environment effectively. This pursuit of growth is not limited to formal education but extends to experiential learning and self-reflection. By engaging in continuous learning, meditating and proclaiming the relevant words of God, individuals equip themselves with the tools necessary to overcome the barriers that once seemed insurmountable.

Another vital aspect is the role of faith and belief in one's journey to transcend limits. Faith, in this context, is not confined to religious connotations but encompasses a deep-seated belief in one's abilities and potential. "For we live by faith, not by sight." – 2 Corinthians 5:7. It is the conviction that, regardless of the circumstances, one has the capacity to achieve their goals. This belief acts as a driving force, motivating individuals to persist in the face of adversity and to continue striving for their aspirations.

Community and support systems also play a significant role in the process of living beyond limits. Surrounding oneself with positive influences and a supportive network of people of strong faith, like Pastors and elders, provides the encouragement and motivation needed during challenging times. These relationships offer perspective, guidance, and reinforcement of the belief that transcending limits is possible. Engaging with a community of like-minded individuals fosters a sense of belonging and shared purpose, which can be instrumental in overcoming personal barriers and cycles of defeat.

Ultimately, the journey to living beyond limits is a personal and ongoing process that requires dedication, resilience, and a willingness to embrace change. It involves a commitment to personal growth and a belief in one's potential based on the word of God to achieve greatness. By adopting a mindset that views limitations as opportunities for growth, individuals can break free from the cycle of defeat and step into a life of boundless possibilities. This transformation is not instantaneous but is achieved through consistent effort and a relentless pursuit of one's dreams and constantly trusting in God, who is trustworthy.

8

Breaking Free from Worry

Understanding Worry

Worry is a pervasive and debilitating force that can infiltrate the mind, causing a cycle of defeat. It often begins with a focus on one's circumstances, drawing attention away from the promises of peace and provision that are available through faith. Philippians 4:6-7 says, "Do not be anxious about anything, but in every situation, by prayer and petition, with thanksgiving, present your requests to God. And the peace of God, which surpasses all understanding, will guard your hearts and minds through Christ Jesus." The process of overcoming worry involves a deliberate shift in focus from the external challenges to the internal assurance of divine support. This transition is not merely a passive acceptance but an active engagement in resisting the strategies of doubt and fear that seek to undermine faith.

The first step in understanding worry involves recognising it as a tactic used to distract and paralyse. Worry thrives when the mind is fixated on the immediate, often overwhelming circumstances, rather than on the broader picture of faith and divine provision. It is crucial to acknowledge that worry is not a natural state of being but a learnt response that can be unlearnt through conscious effort and spiritual discipline. The Word of God in the Bible says in 2 Timothy 1:7 that "For God gave us a spirit not of fear but of power and love and self-control."

To combat worry, one must engage in a practice of casting burdens onto a higher power, i.e., God, trusting that these concerns are being handled with care and wisdom beyond human understanding. The word of God also confirms that "Psalm 55:22: Cast your burden on the Lord, and he will sustain you; he will never permit the righteous to be moved." This act of casting is not a mere dismissal of problems but a strategic release of control, allowing for a peace that surpasses human comprehension to take root. It involves a mental discipline to resist the urge to dwell on the negative and instead cultivate a mindset of faith and expectation.

Moreover, understanding worry requires a shift in perspective from viewing challenges as insurmountable obstacles to seeing them as opportunities for growth and deeper faith. This perspective shift can be facilitated by focusing on past experiences of overcoming and the promises that have been fulfilled. It is essential to remember that worry is a thief of joy and a barrier to receiving the full measure of peace that is available.

In the journey to break free from the cycle of worry, it is helpful to maintain a record of instances where worry has been successfully overcome, serving as a testament to the power of faith and the reliability of divine promises. This practice not only strengthens personal resolve but also provides a tangible reminder of progress and the potential for future victories.

Ultimately, understanding worry is about recognising its transient nature and the power individuals possess to choose a different response. Fear is right when it is reverence toward God because of his holiness (Isa 8:13), and care is good when showing concern for others (1Co 12:25; 2Co 11:28). But worry is always wrong, for itlyzes active faith in your life. When you worry, you assume responsibility for things you were never intended to handle. It is about reclaiming the mind from the grip of fear and doubt and redirecting it towards hope and assurance available in the word of God. Through intentional focus on faith on God and His words, persistent resistance to negative thoughts, and a commitment to viewing challenges as stepping stones rather than stumbling blocks, one can effectively break the cycle of defeat and live a life marked by peace and confidence.

Faith Over Fear

In times of adversity, it is crucial to shift focus from fear to faith. Fear, often amplified by unfavorable circumstances, can cloud judgment and hinder progress. It is a tool of the devil that can be exploited to keep individuals trapped in a cycle of defeat. Overcoming fear requires a conscious effort to redirect one's thoughts and energy toward faith—faith in a higher power i.e. word of God and God of Bible, faith in oneself as what we are in Christ, and faith in the positive outcomes that lie ahead based on that. The scripture emphasizes the importance of maintaining peace amid turmoil as fear paralyze your faith in life's storms, Word of God in Bible is urging believers to trust in divine guidance and protection available through the word of God. This peace is not merely the absence of conflict but a profound sense of assurance that transcends understanding, guarding one's heart and mind against the assaults of fear and doubt. As the word of God in Philippians 4:6-7 say "Be anxious for nothing, but in everything by prayer and supplication, with thanksgiving, let your requests be made known to God; and the peace of God, which surpasses all understanding, will guard your hearts and minds through Christ Jesus".

Embracing faith over fear involves a deliberate choice to focus on positive outcomes rather than potential failures. It requires a steadfast belief in the promises laid out in spiritual teachings of the word of God, which assure victory and deliverance. In John 14:27 Jesus Himself said "Peace I leave with you; my peace I give to you. Not as the world gives do I give to you. Do not let your hearts be troubled or afraid". This shift in perspective is not always easy, as the challenges of life can be overwhelming, much like raging storms threatening to capsize a small boat. However, the key is to remember who is in control and to rely on the strength and wisdom that comes from that knowledge.

The biblical story of the disciples in the storm serves as a powerful illustration. In the biblical story of Jesus calming the storm, Jesus, while sleeping in a boat with his disciples, commands the wind and waves to be still, resulting in a sudden and complete calm. This miracle, recorded in

Matthew 8:23–27, Mark 4:35–41, and Luke 8:22–25, demonstrates Jesus' power over nature and the disciples' subsequent awe and fear. Despite witnessing numerous miracles, the disciples allowed fear to dominate their minds, forgetting the power that was present with them. When Jesus calmed the storm, He questioned their lack of faith, highlighting the need for unwavering trust even in dire circumstances. This narrative underscores the principle that faith, when activated, can bring about peace and resolution, transforming chaos into calm.

In practical terms, living with faith over fear means actively resisting the temptation to dwell on negative thoughts and instead, focusing on the positive aspects of one's situation. It involves casting aside doubts and worries, replacing them with affirmations of faith. This mental discipline is crucial for breaking free from the cycle of defeat. By consistently choosing faith, individuals can find strength and resilience, enabling them to face challenges with confidence and emerge victorious. Rember the great promise of God in Psalm 55:22 "Cast your burden on the Lord, And He shall sustain you; He shall never permit the righteous to be [a]moved".

Moreover, faith is not passive; it requires action. It involves taking steps, however small, towards the desired outcome, trusting that each step is guided and supported. This proactive approach is essential in manifesting the faith that one professes. As faith grows, fear diminishes, and the path to victory becomes clearer. The journey of faith is a continuous process of learning, growing, and trusting, leading to a life characterized by peace and fulfillment.

Ultimately, the message is clear: fear may be a natural response to life's uncertainties, but it should not be the defining force. By choosing faith over fear, individuals can break free from the shackles of defeat and step into a life of victory and purpose. Several Bible verses encourage choosing faith over fear, emphasizing trust in God and His promises. Verses like Isaiah 41:10, Deuteronomy 31:6, and Philippians 4:6-7 offer words of encouragement and guidance in overcoming anxiety and embracing faith. This transformation begins with a conscious decision to trust in the power (can be drawn by trusting on the relevant words of God from Bible) that lies beyond the immediate circumstances, believing in the potential for positive change and the fulfillment of promises. The concept of God never failing is supported by various scriptures, such as Numbers 23:19, Joshua 21:45, and Luke 1:37. He will never fail and will deliver from all fears, provided you exercise faith over fear.

Cultivating Trust in God

In times of uncertainty and adversity, the foundation of trust in God becomes an essential anchor for believers. Hebrews 6:19 states, "We have this as a sure and steadfast anchor of the soul, a hope that enters into that within the veil." This verse emphasizes that our hope in Christ is a secure and dependable anchor for our souls, like an anchor firmly holding a ship steady in a storm. This hope is not just a fleeting feeling, but a solid foundation in Christ, holding us fast in the face of life's trials and uncertainties. Trusting in God requires a deliberate decision to place faith beyond the visible circumstances and into the unseen assurances of divine providence. This trust is not passive; it is an active engagement with faith, a conscious choice to believe in God's promises despite what the physical eyes see. The scriptures remind us that God's plans are inherently good, designed to prosper and uplift, not to harm as confirm the word of God in Jeremiah 29:11 "For I know the thoughts that I think toward you, says the Lord, thoughts of peace and not of evil, to give you a future and a hope. This understanding is the bedrock on which trust is cultivated".

To nurture this trust, one must first acknowledge the sovereignty of God in all situations. Recognizing that no event occurs outside of God's permission allows believers to rest in the assurance that every challenge has a purpose. Several Bible verses offer reassurance that challenges have purpose, allowing believers to find rest in God's plan. Verses like Romans 8:28, Jeremiah 29:11, and Philippians 1:6 express God's overarching purpose and faithfulness, encouraging trust in His guidance, even in difficult times. This perspective shifts focus from the turmoil of circumstances to the steadfastness of God's character. The biblical narrative of Job exemplifies this principle, as he faced immense trials yet maintained his trust in God, affirming that divine wisdom surpasses human understanding.

Furthermore, cultivating trust involves a persistent refusal to succumb to fear and worry, which are tools of the power of darkness that can derail faith. Fear distracts and diminishes the capacity to see God's hand at work. By contrast, trust is fortified by the peace that surpasses understanding—a peace that guards the hearts and minds of those who fix their thoughts on God. And Philippians 4:6-7 "Be anxious for nothing, but in everything by prayer and supplication, with thanksgiving, let your requests be made known to God; and the peace of God, which surpasses all understanding, will guard your hearts and minds through Christ Jesus". This peace acts as a shield against the fiery darts of doubt and anxiety that seek to penetrate the believer's resolve.

A practical step in nurturing trust is through prayer and meditation on God's Word. Engaging with scripture allows believers to internalize God's promises and draw strength from them. Regular prayer fosters a deeper relationship with God, reinforcing trust through communication and divine reassurance. In prayer, believers cast their burdens upon the Lord, releasing the weight of anxiety and embracing the peace of surrender.

Moreover, trust is exemplified in the life of Jesus, who, even in the face of imminent suffering, remained anchored in the Father's will. His example teaches that trust does not eliminate trials but transforms the believer's response to them. Trust empowers believers to declare, like Jesus in the storm, that peace can reign amidst chaos. It is this peace that sustains and propels believers forward, confident in the knowledge that they are never alone.

In essence, cultivating trust in God is a journey of continuous growth and reliance on His faithfulness. It requires a daily commitment to choose faith over fear, to see beyond the immediate and into the eternal. Romans 8:28 says "And we know that in all things God works for the good of those who love him, who have been called according to his purpose." This verse assures believers that God is working all things together for their benefit, encouraging them to trust in His plan.

As believers grow in trust, they find themselves equipped to face life's challenges with courage and hope, assured that God's love and plans for them are unchanging and perfect.

Walking in Assurance

Walking in assurance is an essential element in breaking the cycle of defeat. To achieve this, one must understand that the foundation of assurance is rooted in the knowledge that God is in control of every circumstance. The reality of life is that adversities and trials are inevitable, yet these challenges are not meant to break us but to build our endurance and faith. Recognizing that God allows certain tests to refine and strengthen us is crucial.

The foundation of assurance in the Bible is often rooted in the knowledge of God's unwavering character and promises. Key verses emphasize God's faithfulness, His love, and His presence as the source of comfort and certainty. For example, Philippians 4:6-7 encourages trusting in God's peace, which transcends understanding, and Isaiah 41:10 assures believers that God is with them, strengthening and upholding them.

Assurance comes from the understanding that God's ultimate purpose is to do us good. In every trial, God has provided a way of escape, a provision for victory. This assurance is not the absence of problems but the presence of divine strength to overcome them. It is about shifting focus from the magnitude of the problem to the greatness of God's power and promises. This involves a conscious effort to replace stress with peace, as peace is a powerful antidote to the attacks of worry and fear that often accompany life's challenges.

Replacing stress with peace requires setting the mind on God and His faithfulness. Isaiah 26:3 states, "You will keep in perfect peace those whose minds are steadfast, because they trust in you." This verse emphasizes the importance of trusting in God for a deep and lasting peace, achievable when one's mind is focused on and committed to God. The peace of God guards our hearts and minds, enabling us to face adversities with a calm assurance that God is working everything for our good. This peace is a divine gift that surpasses all understanding (Philippines 4:7), allowing us to remain steadfast even in the most turbulent times.

Moreover, walking in assurance involves rejoicing in trials. The scriptures encourage counting it all joy when faced with various trials, for these are opportunities for our faith to be tested and strengthened. Rejoicing is not about being happy for the trials themselves but for the perfecting work they accomplish within us. It is about praising God, not for the trial, but for His presence and the assurance that He is working through it for our ultimate good.

A key aspect of walking in assurance is taking our eyes off the circumstances and fixing them on Jesus. The core concept of focusing on Jesus instead of circumstances is powerfully expressed in Hebrews 12:2: "Let us fix our eyes on Jesus, the author and perfecter of our faith, who for the joy set before him endured the cross, scorning its shame, and is seated at the right hand of the throne of God." This verse emphasizes that Jesus is the ultimate example to follow and that by fix our eyes on him, we can endure trials with greater perseverance and joy. By focusing on God's promises rather than the problems, we tap into the strength and peace that is available to us. This shift in focus helps us to resist the strategies of Satan, who seeks to use our circumstances to instill fear, worry, and doubt. By aligning our thoughts with God's Word, we break free from the cycle of defeat and enter a cycle of victory.

Ultimately, walking in assurance is about releasing our faith. Hebrews 11:1 "Now faith is the assurance of things hoped for, the conviction of things not seen." This verse defines faith as the foundation upon which we build our hope and assurance, even for things we cannot see or understand. It involves casting all our cares upon God (1Peter 1:7), believing in His covenant promises, and acting on our faith as if we have already received the victory. This proactive faith stance is crucial because it aligns our actions with our beliefs, enabling us to experience the reality of God's promises in our lives. Through faith, we access the peace, strength, and victory that is our inheritance as children of God. In doing so, we break the cycle of defeat and live in the assurance of God's unfailing love and faithfulness.

9

The Power of Prayer

Communicating with God

Communicating with God involves a deep, personal connection that transcends the mundane aspects of daily life. Key verses include "Draw near to God, and he will draw near to you" (James 4:8) and "Call to Me and I will answer you" (Jeremiah 33:3). These verses highlight a reciprocal relationship where seeking God leads to a closer connection. This connection is not solely about speaking to God but also involves listening and being receptive to His guidance. It requires setting aside time to be still and attune oneself to His presence, allowing for a two-way communication that enriches the soul. Psalm 46:10 states, "Be still, and know that I am God." This verse encourages seeking peace and recognizing God's authority. Additionally, Psalms 37:7 suggests waiting patiently and being still in the presence of the Lord, urging trust in His timing. This spiritual exchange forms the foundation of a life aligned with divine purpose and strength.

The process of communicating with God can be compared to tuning into a specific frequency. Just as a radio must be set to the correct channel to receive a clear signal, individuals must clear their minds of distractions and focus intently on God to receive His messages. This involves prayer, meditation, and reflection upon God's Word, which serve as conduits through which His presence and guidance are felt more profoundly.

Prayer serves as a primary means of communication with God. It is not merely a ritualistic practice but a heartfelt conversation that reflects one's innermost thoughts, desires, and concerns. Through prayer, individuals express gratitude, seek forgiveness, and ask for guidance. It is a moment of surrender, where one acknowledges their limitations and relies on God's infinite wisdom and strength.

Listening is an equally important aspect of communicating with God. Isaiah 55:3 says Give ear and come to me; listen, that you may live. I will make an everlasting covenant with you, my faithful love promised to David". This involves being open to receiving messages that may come through various channels, such as scripture, the counsel of others, or even the quiet whisper of intuition. To listen effectively, one must cultivate a sense of inner stillness, creating a space where God's voice can be heard amidst the noise of daily life.

God communicates in ways that are often subtle and require keen spiritual sensitivity to discern. This can include insights or revelations that come during moments of quiet reflection or through the interpretation of life's events. By remaining open and attentive, individuals can perceive the guidance and direction that God provides, helping them navigate the complexities of life with faith and confidence. Just see Isaiah 30:21 "Whether you turn to the right or to the left, your ears will hear a voice behind you, saying, "This is the way; walk in it." And that means that God will guide his people by speaking to them and directing them on the right path, regardless of their choices. The verse promises that when individuals turn to the right or left, they will hear God's voice behind them, saying, "This is the way, walk in it". This verse emphasizes God's consistent and compassionate guidance, assuring individuals that they are never truly alone in their journey of faith and H would is with them.

The relationship with God is strengthened through consistent and earnest communication. As individuals grow in their spiritual journey, they become more attuned to God's presence and more adept at discerning His will. This ongoing dialogue fosters a deep sense of peace and assurance, knowing that one is never alone and that divine support is always available.

Ultimately, communicating with God is about building a relationship that is rooted in love, trust, and faith. It is a dynamic and evolving interaction that requires patience, perseverance, and a willing heart. By prioritizing this divine connection, individuals can break free from the cycle of defeat and live a life marked by victory and fulfillment.

Praying with Purpose

Prayer is a profound tool that empowers individuals to transcend the challenges and adversities they face. It is not merely a ritualistic exercise but a purposeful engagement with the divine. The essence of praying with purpose lies in its ability to align one's will with God's will, thereby transforming circumstances and fostering spiritual growth. This process involves several key elements that work together to break the cycle of defeat and usher in a cycle of victory.

The first element is understanding the nature of prayer as a dialogue with God. It is not a monologue where one merely presents a list of requests. Instead, it is an interactive communication that requires attentiveness to God's voice and guidance. Luke 11:9-13 says "So I say to you, ask, and it will be given to you; seek, and you will find; knock, and it will be opened to you. For everyone who asks receives, and he who seeks finds, and to him who knocks it will be opened. If a son asks for [a]bread from any father among you, will he give him a stone? Or if he asks for a fish, will he give him a serpent instead of a fish? Or if he asks for an egg, will he offer him a scorpion? If you then, being evil, know how to give good gifts to your children, how much more will your heavenly Father give the Holy Spirit to those who ask Him!" This requires a shift from seeking immediate solutions to seeking God's perspective and wisdom. It is about prioritizing divine understanding over personal desires, which ultimately leads to a deeper sense of peace and purpose".

Another critical aspect is the intentional focus on God's promises rather than the present circumstances. Several Bible verses encourage focusing on God's promises even when circumstances seem dire. One example is Hebrews 10:35-36, which emphasizes the importance of holding onto faith despite delays in seeing God's promises fulfilled. Another verse that highlights this concept is Job 42:10, which illustrates Job's endurance through trials and his eventual restoration after focusing on God's promises. This focus shifts the believer's mindset from one of defeat to one of victory. By concentrating on the assurances provided in the scriptures, individuals can anchor their faith in the certainty of God's plan and purpose for their lives. This faith is not passive; it demands active participation in believing that God's promises will manifest in due time. Hebrews 11:1 which defines faith as "assurance of things hoped for, the conviction of things not seen". Mark 11:22-25 illustrates faith in action, urging believers to have faith in God and to believe that what they ask in prayer will be given to them.

Moreover, praying with purpose involves releasing control and trusting in God's sovereignty. It requires relinquishing the need to dictate the outcomes and instead, resting in the knowledge that God's plan is perfect. Verses like Proverbs 3:5-6, Jeremiah 29:11, and Philippians 4:6-7 encourage faith, surrendering plans, and trusting God's will. Verses like Romans 8:28 remind us that God works all things together for good for those who love Him. This surrender is not a sign of weakness but a testament to one's faith in God's omnipotence. It is about acknowledging that while one may not understand the journey, God is orchestrating every detail for ultimate good.

In addition, praying with purpose necessitates a heart of gratitude. Even in the face of trials, maintaining a posture of thankfulness shifts the focus from what is lacking to what has been provided. Several Bible passages emphasize maintaining thankfulness even amidst trials. 1 Thessalonians 5:18 instructs, "Give thanks in every circumstance; for this is God's will for you in Christ Jesus". Philippians 4:6 encourages, "Do not be anxious about anything, but in every situation, by prayer and petition, with thanksgiving, present your requests to God". These verses highlight the importance of expressing gratitude not just in good times, but also when facing challenges. Gratitude fosters a positive outlook, which is essential in overcoming the negative emotions that often accompany challenging circumstances. It is through gratitude that individuals can find joy and contentment, regardless of external conditions.

Finally, persistent prayer is a hallmark of praying with purpose. It is the steadfast commitment to continue seeking God, even when answers are delayed or when the path forward seems unclear. This persistence is not about changing God's mind but rather about transforming the individual's heart and aligning it more closely with God's desires. 1 Thessalonians 5:17 say that "Pray without ceasing." This verse encourages constant communication with God, fostering a spiritual connection that provides strength and resilience. Through persistent prayer, individuals build spiritual resilience and fortitude, enabling them to withstand life's storms.

In conclusion, praying with purpose is a dynamic and transformative practice that empowers individuals to break free from the cycle of defeat. By engaging in purposeful prayer, believers can experience profound spiritual growth, align their lives with God's will, and live victoriously amidst life's challenges.

Receiving God's Promises

In the pursuit of breaking the cycle of defeat, one must understand the significance of receiving God's promises. This process involves both understanding and applying the principles that God has set forth in His Word. The first step is to recognize that God's promises are available to everyone who believes (John 3:16 & John 1:12-13). These promises are not limited by human understanding or circumstances but are based on the unchanging nature of God as expressed in His word in Hebrew 6:17 "Because God wanted to make the unchanging nature of his purpose very clear to the heirs of what was promised, he confirmed it with an oath". His Word is a covenant, a binding agreement that He will fulfill.

To receive these promises, it is essential to align one's heart and mind with God's truth. This means letting go of doubt and embracing faith. Doubt is a tool that Satan uses to keep believers trapped in a cycle of defeat. By planting seeds of doubt, he aims to make individuals question God's love and His covenant promises. The antidote to this is unwavering faith, which is built through a deep relationship with God and an understanding of His Word. A verse that emphasizes unwavering faith is Hebrews 10:23, which says,

"Let us hold fast the confession of our hope without wavering, for He who promised is faithful." This verse encourages believers to hold firmly to the hope they profess, relying on God's faithfulness rather than their own fluctuating emotions or circumstances.

The Bible teaches that faith comes by hearing, and hearing by the Word of God (Roman 10:17). Therefore, immersing oneself in the Scriptures is crucial. This involves more than just reading; it requires meditating on the Word, allowing it to penetrate the heart and transform the mind. As believers grow in their knowledge of God's promises, they build a strong foundation of faith that can withstand the attacks of the enemy.

Prayer is another vital component in receiving God's promises. It is through prayer that believers communicate with God, express their needs, and receive divine guidance. Prayer should be accompanied by thanksgiving (Philippians 4:6-7), as it demonstrates trust in God's provision and faithfulness. When believers pray with a heart full of gratitude, they position themselves to receive God's promises with open hearts.

Moreover, it is important to act on what one believes. Faith without works is dead (James 2:26) as stated in the Scriptures. To receive God's promises, believers must live as though those promises have already been fulfilled. This active faith demonstrates to God that they truly believe in His Word and His ability to deliver on His promises.

In times of trial, it is crucial to remain steadfast and patient. God's timing is perfect, and His plans are always for the good of those who love Him. During these times, believers should focus on God's faithfulness in the past and trust that He will continue to fulfill His promises in the future.

Lastly, believers must resist the temptation to rely on their own understanding. Human reasoning can often be a stumbling block to faith. Instead, trust should be placed entirely in God, who is able to do exceedingly abundantly above all that one can ask or think (Ephesian 3:20). Proverbs 3:5-6 "Trust in the Lord with all your heart and lean not on your own understanding. In all your ways submit to him, and he will make your paths straight". By fully surrendering to God and His promises, believers will experience the victory that comes from living in alignment with His will.

Transformative Prayer

Transformative prayer stands as a powerful tool for believers seeking to break free from cycles of defeat. It is a dynamic process that involves a deep connection with the divine, allowing individuals to transcend their immediate circumstances and align themselves with a higher purpose. At its core, transformative prayer is about surrender and trust in a divine plan that surpasses human understanding.

The first step in engaging in transformative prayer is to approach it with an open heart and mind. This means letting go of preconceived notions and allowing oneself to be vulnerable before God. It is in this vulnerability that true transformation begins, as it opens the door for divine intervention and guidance. By acknowledging one's limitations and placing trust in a higher power i.e. on God and His promises, individuals can begin to see their challenges from a new perspective.

In transformative prayer, the focus shifts from the problem at hand to the possibilities that lie beyond it. This shift in focus is crucial as it helps to break the cycle of defeat by redirecting energy towards positive outcomes and divine solutions. Instead of dwelling on the negative aspects of a situation, transformative prayer encourages believers to envision the positive changes that can occur through faith and divine intervention.

Another critical aspect of transformative prayer is the element of thanksgiving. By expressing gratitude for the blessings that one has, even in the midst of trials, individuals can cultivate a mindset of abundance and positivity. This gratitude serves as a reminder of God's faithfulness and the countless ways in which He has already intervened in one's life. It reinforces the belief that, regardless of the current circumstances, God is working behind the scenes to bring about a greater good.

Moreover, transformative prayer involves a commitment to continuous spiritual growth. It is not a one-time event but an ongoing journey of deepening one's relationship with God. This commitment requires discipline and dedication, as it involves regular prayer, meditation on God and His words, and reflection. Through these practices, individuals can strengthen their faith and develop a greater understanding of God's will for their lives.

Several Bible verses emphasize the transformative power of prayer. Verses like Romans 12:2 and 2 Corinthians 3:18 highlight the renewing of the mind and being transformed into God's image through prayer. Other verses, such as Philippians 4:6-7, encourage prayer with thanksgiving and emphasize the peace that transcends understanding, which can guard the heart and mind.

Furthermore, transformative prayer is characterized by a sense of peace and assurance. As believers place their trust in God, they experience a profound sense of calm, knowing that they are not alone in their struggles. This peace is a testament to the power of prayer to transcend human limitations and connect individuals with a divine source of strength and wisdom.

Ultimately, transformative prayer is about empowerment. It empowers individuals to rise above their circumstances and embrace a life of victory and purpose. By aligning oneself with God's will, believers can overcome the obstacles that stand in their way and experience the fullness of life that God intends for them. It is through this transformative process that individuals can break free from cycles of defeat and step into a new reality of hope and possibility.

10

Living in God's Promises

Understanding God's Covenant

The concept of God's covenant is central to understanding the relationship between the divine and humanity. A covenant, in its biblical context, is a solemn agreement or promise between God and His people, characterized by commitments and obligations on both sides. Deuteronomy 7:9 says that "Know therefore that the Lord your God is God; he is the faithful God, keeping his covenant of love to a thousand generations of those who love him and keep his commandments". This divine agreement is not merely a contract; it is a profound bond that assures believers of God's unending faithfulness and love. 2 Timothy 2:13 explains that "If we are faithless, he remains faithful, for he cannot deny himself."

Throughout history, God has made several covenants with humanity, each serving as a testament to His desire for a deep and enduring relationship with His creation. One key verse is Numbers 23:19, which states, "God is not a man, that He should lie, nor a son of man, that He should repent; has He said, and will He not do it? Or has He spoken, and will He not make it good?" These covenants are pivotal in breaking the cycle of defeat that many individuals face in their spiritual and daily lives. By understanding and embracing God's covenant, believers can access the strength and peace necessary to overcome adversity.

One of the key aspects of God's covenant is its everlasting nature. Unlike human agreements, which can be broken or altered, God's covenant is unchangeable and eternal. This is beautifully illustrated in the covenant made with Abraham (Gensis 12:1-3), where God promised to bless him and make his descendants as numerous as the stars. This promise was a declaration of God's unwavering commitment to His people and a demonstration of His power to fulfill His word, irrespective of circumstances.

Moreover, God's covenant is marked by His promises to provide, protect, and prosper His people. Psalm 23:1: "The Lord is my shepherd; I shall not want. In the covenant with Israel, God assured them of His protection and provision as long as they remained faithful to His commandments. This assurance is not limited to material blessings but extends to spiritual enrichment and peace, which are crucial in overcoming the challenges of life.

God's covenant also involves a call to obedience and faith. Many examples in the Bible illustrate the connection between faith and obedience, such as Noah building the ark (Genesis 6-7) or Abraham's willingness to sacrifice Isaac (Genesis 22). It requires believers to trust in God's promises and align their lives with His will. This trust is not passive; it is an active engagement with God's word and a steadfast belief in His ability to deliver on His promises. When believers hold fast to their part of the covenant, they position themselves to experience God's faithfulness in profound ways. Obedience, therefore, becomes a visible expression of faith. It shows that God's word is trusted and followed, even when it requires sacrifice or goes against what humans may expect.

In the New Testament, the covenant takes on a new dimension with the coming of Jesus Christ. Through His sacrifice, Jesus established a new covenant, sealed with His blood, offering redemption and eternal life to all who believe. The New Covenant, established through Jesus, emphasizes the importance of faith in Christ for forgiveness and reconciliation with God, but it also calls for ongoing obedience in obedience to God's will. This new covenant emphasizes grace and forgiveness, providing believers with the assurance of salvation and the empowerment to live victorious lives.

Understanding God's covenant is crucial for breaking the cycle of defeat. Jeremiah 31:31-34 "This verse introduces the concept of a new covenant, where God will write His law on the hearts of His people and forgive their sins, offering a path to a more profound and lasting relationship with Him". It equips believers with the knowledge that they are not alone in their struggles and that God is actively working to bring about their good. By embracing the covenant of God, individuals can move from a place of defeat to a life characterized by victory and peace. God's covenant is a reminder of His unyielding love and His desire for His people to thrive in every aspect of their lives.

Isaiah 54:10: "Though the mountains be shaken and the hills be removed, yet my unfailing love for you will not be shaken nor my covenant of peace be removed," says the LORD, who has compassion on you." This verse speaks to the enduring nature of God's love and covenant, even amidst hardship. By standing on the promises of God's covenant, believers can confidently face any challenge, knowing that victory is assured through His divine grace and power.

Faithful Living

Faithful living is an essential aspect of breaking the cycle of defeat. It involves aligning one's life with principles that foster resilience and spiritual strength in the face of adversity. The process begins with understanding the role of faith in overcoming life's challenges. Romans 1:17 "This verse states that "the righteous will live by faith." It highlights that faith is the driving force behind a believer's life and conduct. Faith is not merely a passive belief but an active force that propels individuals to trust in divine provision available in Bible and guidance, even when circumstances seem unfavorable.

Central to faithful living is the concept of peace, which serves as a counterbalance to the stress and turmoil that often accompany life's trials. When facing adversity, it is crucial to replace stress with peace by focusing on God's faithfulness and allowing Christ's peace to guard one's heart and mind. Jesus promised in John 14:27 "Peace I leave with you; my peace I give you. I do not give to you as the world gives. Do not let your hearts be troubled and do not be afraid". This peace is not a mere absence of conflict but a profound sense of well-being that comes from trusting in God's words and the everlasting strength available through it.

Another key element is the attitude of rejoicing in trials. God words proclaim in Romans 12:12 "Rejoice in hope, be patient in tribulation, be constant in prayer". This perspective shifts the focus from the pain of the trial to the growth and endurance it produces. By rejoicing, individuals partake in Christ's sufferings, knowing that these experiences refine their character and increase their capacity for joy when His glory is revealed.

Moreover, faithful living requires a deliberate effort to take one's eyes off the immediate circumstances and fix them on Jesus and God's Word. This shift in focus allows individuals to rise above the challenges and see their situations from a divine perspective. Hebrews 12:2 "looking unto Jesus, the author and finisher of our faith, who for the joy that was set before Him endured the cross, despising the shame, and has sat down at the right hand of the throne of God". It involves laying aside every burden and sin that easily ensnares and running the race with patience, looking unto Jesus, the author and finisher of faith. This verse highlights that suffering, though painful, can lead to positive character development.

Resisting the adversary is another crucial aspect of faithful living. James 4:7, which instructs believers to "submit to God and resist the devil," promising that he will flee. Victory over life's circumstances does not come automatically but requires active participation in spiritual warfare. Ephesians 6:11, This verse uses the powerful imagery of the armor of God, emphasizing that believers are not just fighting flesh and blood, but spiritual wickedness in high places. It encourages believers to equip themselves spiritually to stand firm against the devil's schemes. God has equipped believers with armor to protect them and powerful weapons to take authority over the enemy. It is essential to recognize that the moment fear, worry, or doubt attacks the mind, these must be cast out in the Name of Jesus, binding the enemy's work in the circumstances.

Faithful living also involves releasing one's faith through prayer. "Casting all cares upon Jesus" and believing in God's care is rooted in the Bible, particularly in 1 Peter 5:7. This means casting all cares upon Jesus and believing in God's covenant promises. It requires acting on faith as if the answer has already been received, even before seeing any evidence of it as mentioned in Mark 11:24 "Therefore I tell you, whatever you ask in prayer, believe that you have received it, and it will be yours.". Such unwavering faith is essential for breaking the cycle of defeat and entering a cycle of victory.

Finally, perseverance in faithful living is vital. Hebrews 10:36 "You need to persevere so that when you have done the will of God, you will receive what he has promised". Regardless of how long one has waited for deliverance or the intensity of the pain, perseverance in the Spirit is necessary. This involves continuous prayer, belief, and the expectation of God's deliverance. By maintaining this stance, individuals can overcome the strategies of the enemy and live in a cycle of victory, free from the defeat that once ensnared them.

Overcoming Through Promises

Hebrews 10:23 encourages believers to "hold fast the confession of our hope without wavering, for he who promised is faithful". Promises are often seen as commitments that provide a sense of assurance and hope. In the context of overcoming cycles of defeat, promises carry profound significance as they become the foundation upon which faith and perseverance are built. The power of promises lies not just in their words but in the trust and expectation they generate. When individuals face challenging circumstances, the promises of God they hold onto serve as beacons of light, guiding them through the darkest times.

The journey of breaking free from defeat begins with understanding that promises are not mere words but are backed by a God. In Joshua 23:14: the word of God says that "You know with all your heart and soul that not one of all the good promises the LORD your God has given you has failed. Not one of them has failed." They are assurances of support, guidance, and eventual victory. Isaiah 55:11 says that "So is my word that goes out from my mouth: It will not return to me empty, but will accomplish what I desire and achieve the purpose for which I sent it." It is essential to recognize that these promises, especially those grounded in spiritual or divine contexts, are meant to be sources of strength. They remind individuals that there is a purpose behind every trial and that enduring these trials leads to personal growth and eventual triumph.

The word God explains in 2 Corinthians 1:6-7 "If we are afflicted, it is for your comfort and salvation, and if we are comforted, it is for your comfort and salvation. If we are afflicted, we suffer for you, and if we are comforted, we comfort you. We know that God can comfort you as we have been comforted in all our afflictions."

In practical terms, overcoming through promises involves a few critical steps. First, it is crucial to identify and internalize the promises that are relevant to one's life and circumstances. This can be achieved by reflecting on personal beliefs, values, and the assurances provided by one's faith or support system. Once these promises are identified, they must be internalized and believed in wholeheartedly. This belief is what transforms promises from mere words into powerful motivators that fuel resilience and determination.

Another key aspect of overcoming through promises is the active application of these promises in daily life. To actively apply God's promises in daily life, consider verses like Proverbs 3:5-6 ("Trust in the Lord with all your heart and lean not on your own understanding; in all your ways submit to him, and he will make your paths straight.") This involves making conscious decisions that align with the promises one holds dear. For example, if a promise assures victory over adversity, then every action and thought should reflect a mindset of victory rather than defeat. This alignment between belief and action creates a powerful

116

synergy that propels individuals forward, even when faced with seemingly insurmountable obstacles.

Furthermore, it is important to surround oneself with a community that reinforces these promises. Being part of a supportive network provides encouragement and accountability, helping individuals stay focused on their path to overcoming defeat. Sharing experiences and testimonies of how promises have been fulfilled in the past can inspire and reinforce the belief in their power.

Lastly, patience and perseverance are essential components of realizing the fulfillment of promises. While the journey may be fraught with challenges and setbacks, holding onto the promises with unwavering faith ensures that individuals remain steadfast. It is during these times that promises serve as anchors, preventing individuals from being swept away by waves of doubt and despair.

In conclusion, overcoming through claiming, the promises of the God is a dynamic process that involves recognizing, believing, and acting upon the assurances that guide one's life. These promises of the God, when embraced fully, become the catalysts for breaking free from cycles of defeat, leading to a life marked by victory and fulfillment. They are the threads that weave resilience and hope into the fabric of everyday life, empowering individuals to rise above their circumstances and achieve their highest potential.

Victory in God's Word

The idea that victory in life is found through understanding and applying God's Word is central to many Christian beliefs. Verses like 1 Corinthians 15:57 and Romans 8:37 speak to the victory given through faith in Jesus. Victory over life's challenges is deeply rooted in understanding and applying God's Word. The Word of God is not merely a collection of ancient texts but a living, active force that can transform and empower believers to overcome any cycle of defeat. The significance of God's Word lies in its ability to provide guidance, strength, and assurance, helping believers navigate through life's adversities with faith and confidence. John 1:14 "And the Word became flesh and dwelt among us, and we have seen his glory, glory as of the only Son from the Father, full of grace and truth." The words of God in Bible are living word of God and are powerful.

The first step towards victory is acknowledging the power inherent in the scriptures/word of God. God's Word is described as sharper than a double-edged sword, capable of penetrating the deepest parts of our being and discerning our thoughts and intentions (Hebrew 4:12). This understanding encourages believers to immerse themselves in scripture/word of the God, allowing it to shape their thoughts, attitudes, and actions. By doing so, they align themselves with divine wisdom and strength, enabling them to face challenges with a renewed perspective.

Moreover, the Word of God serves as a source of unwavering truth in a world filled with uncertainties and deceit as stated in Proverbs 30:5: "Every word of God is tested; He is a shield to those who trust in him.". It provides a solid foundation upon which believers can build their lives, ensuring that they remain steadfast even when faced with trials. The scriptures remind us that God's promises are sure and His plans for us are good, giving believers hope and a future. Psalm 119:160 says that "All your words are true; all your righteous laws are eternal." This assurance is crucial in breaking the cycle of defeat, as it instills a deep-seated belief that victory is not only possible but guaranteed for those who trust in God's Word.

In addition to being a source of truth and guidance, God's Word is also a powerful weapon against the adversary. Satan's primary strategy is to instill doubt, fear, and defeat in the hearts of believers by distorting the truth and magnifying their problems. Ephesians 6:17 says "And take the helmet of salvation and the sword of the Spirit, which is the word of God." However, by holding fast to the Word of God, believers can counter these attacks, declaring God's promises over their lives and situations. Isaiah 41:10 says ("Fear not, for I am with you"). This act of faith by trusting on the word of God, not only we can silences the enemy but also fortifies believers, enabling them to stand firm in the face of adversity.

Furthermore, the application of God's Word in daily life is essential for maintaining victory. Let us be doers and not just hearers of God's Word (James 1:22). It is not enough to merely read or hear the Word; believers must also live it out. This involves meditating on scripture, confessing it regularly, and allowing it to influence every aspect of their lives. As they do so, they experience the transformative power of the Word, which renews their minds, strengthens their faith, and equips them to overcome any challenge.

The journey to breaking the cycle of defeat and entering a cycle of victory is a continual process of engaging with God's Word. It requires a commitment to studying, understanding, and applying scripture in every situation.

In Hebrews 13:20-21 the word of Gods says "Now may the God of peace, who through the blood of the eternal covenant brought back from the dead our Lord Jesus, that great Shepherd of the sheep, equip you with everything good for doing his will, and may he work in us what is pleasing to him, through Jesus Christ, to whom be glory for ever and ever." This passage emphasizes God's power to equip us with everything we need to fulfill His will.

By doing so, believers not only gain victory over their circumstances but also grow in their relationship with God, experiencing His peace, joy, and strength in abundance. Several Bible verses emphasize the power of God's Word in achieving victory and freedom from defeat. Verses like Hebrews 4:12, John 17:17, and Colossians 3:16 highlight the Word's ability to reveal truth, guide actions, and empower believers to live victorious lives. Ultimately, the Word of God is the key to living a victorious life, free from the chains of defeat.

11

The Battle Against Doubt

Recognising Doubt

In the realm of spiritual growth, recognizing the presence of doubt is a crucial step toward breaking free from the cycle of defeat. Doubt, a subtle yet powerful force, often infiltrates the mind, masking itself as a natural reaction to life's challenges. The word of God in James 1:5-8 "Highlights the importance of asking God for wisdom and emphasizing that a doubter, being unstable, will not receive anything from the Lord, However, it is imperative to understand that doubt is a strategy deliberately employed to weaken resolve and paralyze faith.

To comprehend doubt's impact, one must first acknowledge its origin. Doubt often stems from focusing too intently on circumstances rather than the assurances provided by faith. When life's storms rage, the natural inclination is to fixate on the immediate turmoil, much like the disciples who were overwhelmed by the tempestuous sea despite being in the presence of Christ. In Matthew 14:31 "Jesus confronted Peter's doubt after walking on water, reminding him of his "little faith". Their inability to look beyond the storm to the calming presence of Jesus serves as an allegory for how doubt can cloud judgment and obscure faith. Mathew 8:25: "And he said to them, 'Why are you afraid, you of little faith?' Then he rose and rebuked the winds and the sea, and there was a great calm." We are not to doubt but trust on Him.

The fixation on circumstances allows doubt to flourish, manifesting as fear and anxiety. It is during these moments of vulnerability that doubt whispers its most insidious lies: questioning one's worthiness, God's intentions, and the validity of His promises. These doubts can become so pervasive that they choke the very life out of the faith required to overcome adversities. The cycle of defeat is perpetuated as doubt leads to inaction, and inaction results in stagnation. In James 1:6-7 also the word of God confirms that "But let him ask in faith, without any doubting, for he who doubts is like a wave of the sea, that is driven and tossed about by the wind. That man ought not to think that he will receive anything from the Lord." This verse highlights how doubt can hinder our ability to receive God's blessings.

Breaking free from this cycle necessitates a conscious effort to shift focus from circumstances to faith on God and His words. This involves an intentional act of casting one's worries onto a God (1Peter 1:7) understanding that this act is not a passive relinquishment but an active declaration of trust. It requires the individual to resist the inclination to dwell on the problem and instead embrace the peace that comes from trusting in divine provision and timing by trusting on the word of God.

Moreover, recognizing doubt is not about denying its existence but about confronting it with truth. This truth is found in the assurances of faith, which promise that no trial is insurmountable and no situation is beyond redemption. By anchoring oneself in these truths, the grip of doubt is loosened, allowing for the activation of faith. Hebrews 11:1 says "Now faith is the assurance of things hoped for, the conviction of things not seen." When faith is active, it transforms the perception of circumstances from insurmountable obstacles to opportunities for growth and divine intervention.

In this journey of recognizing and overcoming doubt, it is essential to cultivate a mindset that is vigilant against the encroachments of fear and worry. This vigilance involves nurturing a mental environment where faith can flourish unimpeded by the shadows of doubt. It is about creating a space where the mind is protected by peace and fortified by the knowledge that every challenge is an opportunity for divine demonstration.

Ultimately, recognizing doubt is about reclaiming control over one's spiritual narrative. It is about choosing to see beyond the immediate chaos to the potential for peace and victory. By doing so, one not only breaks the cycle of defeat but also steps into a cycle of continual growth and unwavering faith.

Strengthening Faith

In the pursuit of overcoming life's challenges, one fundamental aspect is the fortification of faith. It is essential to recognize that faith acts as a stabilizing force, providing the strength and assurance needed to face adversities. Hebrews 11:1 says "Faith is the substance of things hoped for" hence we need to strengthen our faith. The process of strengthening faith involves several key actions that can transform one's spiritual journey. Initially, it is crucial to shift focus from the immediate circumstances to the promises of God. This involves a conscious decision to look beyond the visible challenges and to trust in the unseen but ever-present divine support available through the word of God. By doing so, individuals can cultivate a mindset that is resilient and unwavering in the face of trials.

Moreover, the practice of rejoicing in the midst of trials is a powerful method to enhance faith. "Rejoice in the Lord always" is a powerful and encouraging biblical concept, primarily found in Philippians 4:4. It means to find joy and delight in the Lord, regardless of circumstances. This concept, although counterintuitive, is rooted in the understanding that trials are opportunities for growth and development. By embracing joy during difficult times, individuals align themselves with a perspective that acknowledges God's control and purpose in every situation. Rejoicing becomes a declaration of faith, a testament to the belief that God is working all things together for good.

Another critical component in strengthening faith is the active resistance against negative influences that aim to weaken it. This involves a proactive stance against fear, doubt, and worry, which are often used as tools to undermine faith. By resisting these negative emotions and replacing them with thoughts of peace and trust found in word of God, individuals can maintain a strong and vibrant faith. This resistance is not passive but requires a deliberate effort to align one's thoughts with the truth of God's Word.

Prayer and meditation on scripture are also vital practices in this process. Through prayer, individuals can cast their anxieties onto God, allowing His peace to guard their hearts and minds. Meditation on scripture reinforces the promises of God, serving as a constant reminder of His faithfulness and love. These spiritual disciplines help to deepen one's understanding of God, fostering a more intimate relationship with Him.

Lastly, acting on faith is essential. It is not enough to merely believe; faith must be demonstrated through actions. The core idea that "faith without action is dead" is primarily found in the book of James, specifically in James 2:17. This involves making decisions and taking steps that reflect trust in God's promises. Whether it is stepping out in faith to pursue a new opportunity or standing firm in the face of adversity, actions that are rooted in faith serve to strengthen it further. By consistently acting in faith, individuals build a solid foundation that can withstand the pressures and challenges of life.

In conclusion, strengthening faith is a dynamic and ongoing process that requires intentionality and commitment. By focusing on God, rejoicing in trials, resisting negative influences, engaging in prayer and scripture, and acting on faith, individuals can cultivate a robust and enduring faith. This strengthened faith not only provides the resilience needed to overcome life's challenges but also brings about a deeper, more fulfilling relationship with God.

The Role of Belief

Belief plays a pivotal role in breaking free from cycles of defeat. It is the foundation upon which one's journey to victory is built, acting as both a shield and a weapon against the adversities that life presents. The power of belief enables individuals to transcend their immediate circumstances, providing strength and resilience in the face of trials and challenges.

Belief is not merely a passive state of mind; it is an active force that requires nurturing and reinforcement. It demands a conscious decision to trust in a God and His words, to place faith in something greater than oneself. This trust is not blind, but rather informed by the understanding that there is a purpose and a plan beyond what is immediately visible. It is this understanding that fuels the courage to face difficulties head-on, knowing that they are not insurmountable barriers, but stepping stones to personal growth and fulfillment.

In the context of overcoming defeat, belief acts as a catalyst for change. It empowers individuals to shift their focus from the obstacles they encounter to the possibilities that lie beyond them. By fostering a mindset of positivity and hope, belief encourages proactive behavior, prompting individuals to take steps towards their goals with confidence and determination. This proactive stance is essential in breaking negative cycles, as it transforms passive acceptance into active engagement with one's circumstances.

Moreover, belief cultivates resilience, a crucial trait for enduring and overcoming life's challenges. It instills a sense of perseverance, enabling individuals to withstand setbacks and continue striving towards their objectives. This resilience is not a denial of reality, but rather a refusal to be defined by it. It is the strength to rise after a fall, to learn from failure, and to persist despite adversity. Through belief, individuals can maintain their focus on the bigger picture, understanding that temporary setbacks are part of a larger, more meaningful journey.

The role of belief is also evident in its ability to inspire others. When individuals embody a strong belief system, they become beacons of hope and inspiration for those around them. Their unwavering faith and positive outlook can motivate others to adopt similar mindsets, creating a ripple effect of empowerment and change. This collective belief can foster communities of support and encouragement, where individuals uplift one another and work together to overcome shared challenges.

In essence, belief is a transformative power that can liberate individuals from cycles of defeat, guiding them towards a path of victory and fulfillment. It is the inner conviction that fuels perseverance, inspires action, and ignites the potential within each person to overcome obstacles and achieve greatness. By embracing belief, individuals can unlock the strength and resilience needed to navigate the complexities of life, ultimately breaking free from the chains of defeat and stepping boldly into a future defined by possibility and success.

Conquering Uncertainty

In the face of life's inevitable uncertainties, there lies a profound opportunity for growth and transformation. While uncertainty can often evoke fear and hesitation, it is within these moments of unpredictability that individuals can discover their true resilience and strength. The key to navigating uncertainty lies in understanding its nature and developing strategies to effectively confront it with the truth found in the word of God.

Uncertainty is an inherent part of the human experience, affecting every aspect of life, from personal decisions to global events. It can manifest as doubt in one's abilities, unpredictability in relationships, or instability in the world at large. However, it is crucial to recognize that uncertainty is not inherently negative; rather, it serves as a catalyst for innovation and adaptation. By shifting perspective, one can view uncertainty as a landscape filled with potential opportunities waiting to be explored. Psalm 16:1 say "Keep me safe, O God, for in you I take refuge. I said to the LORD, "You are my Lord; apart from you I have no good thing."" This verse highlights the need for protection and trust in God, even in times of uncertainty.

The first step in conquering uncertainty is to cultivate a mindset of acceptance and openness. Embracing uncertainty means reframing it from a source of anxiety to a space of possibility. This involves acknowledging that while not all variables can be controlled, one can control their response to them. Developing emotional resilience through practices such as mindfulness and meditation on the relevant word of God can help ground individuals, allowing them to remain calm and centered amidst chaos.

Furthermore, setting clear goals and maintaining a flexible approach is essential. While it is important to have a direction, adaptability is crucial in adjusting plans as situations evolve. This flexibility enables individuals to pivot when necessary, seizing new opportunities that may arise unexpectedly. By maintaining a balance between steadfastness in purpose and adaptability in method, one can navigate through uncertainty with confidence.

Building a strong support system is another vital strategy. Surrounding oneself with supportive individuals who offer encouragement and diverse perspectives can provide a buffer against the challenges posed by uncertainty. Engaging in open dialogues with trusted friends, mentors, or colleagues can foster a sense of community and shared understanding, which can be incredibly reassuring during tumultuous times.

Moreover, developing problem-solving skills is indispensable in addressing uncertainty. This involves honing critical thinking abilities to analyze situations, identify potential risks, and devise effective solutions. By approaching problems with a strategic mindset, individuals can transform uncertainties into manageable challenges, thereby reducing feelings of helplessness.

Lastly, fostering a spirit of curiosity and continuous learning can empower individuals to thrive in uncertain environments. By remaining curious and open to new information, individuals can expand their knowledge and adapt to changing circumstances more effectively. This proactive approach not only mitigates the impact of uncertainty but also enhances one's capacity for innovation and growth.

In conclusion, while uncertainty is an unavoidable aspect of life, it need not be paralyzing. Psalm 16:1 says "Keep me safe, O God, for in you I take refuge." This verse highlights the importance of trusting in God's protection even when facing uncertainty. By adopting a mindset of acceptance, maintaining flexibility, building supportive networks, and enhancing problem-solving skills, individuals can transform uncertainty into a powerful force for personal and professional development. Embracing uncertainty with courage and curiosity can lead to profound insights and opportunities, ultimately breaking the cycle of defeat and paving the way for a more resilient and fulfilling life in Lord.

12

Walking in Continuous Victory

The Path to Victory

In the pursuit of overcoming life's challenges, it is essential to understand the dynamics that lead to victory over defeat. This involves a strategic approach to transforming one's mindset and actions in the face of adversity. The first step is to replace stress with peace. Bible words in Isaiah 26:3 says "You will keep in perfect peace him whose mind is steadfast, because he trusts in you." This verse emphasizes the connection between a steadfast mind, trust in God, and experiencing God's perfect peace. When confronted with difficult circumstances, it is important to focus on a God relevant word suits to your need, faithfulness rather than succumbing to stress. This shift in trusting God and His word in Bible, allows peace to guard one's heart and mind, fostering a sense of calmness and stability as mentioned in Philippians 4:7-8.

Joy plays a crucial role in navigating trials and temptations. Nehemiah 8:10: "and do not be grieved, for the joy of the Lord is your strength". This verse reminds us that God's joy can be a source of strength and endurance during difficult times. Embracing joy, even in difficult times, is a powerful strategy that aligns with spiritual teachings. It is encouraged to rejoice, as this act not only uplifts the spirit but also aligns with the belief that challenges are part of a greater plan for growth and development.

Another key aspect is redirecting focus from immediate circumstances to a broader perspective rooted in faith on God and scripture (His word). By doing so, individuals can find strength and resilience, drawing inspiration from spiritual figures who endured hardships yet remained steadfast in their beliefs. This approach empowers individuals to resist negative influences and maintain a positive outlook.

Resistance (James 4:7) is vital in combating the strategies that aim to keep one in a cycle of defeat. Employing spiritual armor (Ephesian 6:11) and powerful tools of faith enables individuals to take authority over negative forces. This proactive stance is crucial in preventing negative thoughts, tempting thoughts coming from the enemy, from taking root and affecting one's, corrupting mental and emotional well-being.

Faith is the cornerstone of victory. But thanks be to God, who gives us the victory through our Lord Jesus Christ (1 Corinthians 15:57). It involves casting all worries and concerns upon a God (1 Peter 5:7), trusting in promises found in Bible that provide strength and assurance. Acting on this faith on God and in his word as though the desired outcome has already been achieved is a testament to unwavering belief and conviction (Mark 11:23-24). This mindset not only fosters peace but also strengthens one's resolve in the face of adversity.

Ultimately, the path to victory is paved with a deep understanding of one's spiritual resources found in Bible promises and the personal commitment to apply them in daily life. By replacing stress with peace, embracing joy, redirecting focus, resisting negative influences, and grounding oneself in faith, individuals can break free from cycles of defeat and enter a realm of continuous victory. This journey is not merely about overcoming challenges but about transforming one's entire approach to life, ensuring that every step is guided by a profound sense of purpose and peace. Remember 1 John 5:4 "For whatever is born of God overcomes the world. And this is the victory that has overcome the world— our faith". This verse connects faith with overcoming the world. It suggests that the victory that overcomes the world is not achieved through human effort but through faith in God

Sustaining Success

Achieving and maintaining success is a multifaceted endeavor that requires strategic planning and consistent effort. The key to sustaining success in achieving victory lies in understanding the dynamics that can potentially disrupt it and implementing measures to counteract these forces like trusting on God instead of self. One critical aspect is recognizing that success is not a static destination but a continuous journey that demands adaptability and resilience.

The Bible emphasizes that victory and success depend not on our own strength or understanding, but on God's power and guidance. Verses like Proverbs 21:31, Romans 8:37, and Philippians 4:13 highlight the importance of trusting in God and relying on his resources rather than self-reliance.

Here's a more detailed look at how the Bible addresses this theme: Trusting God for Victory: -

Proverbs 21:31: "The horse is made ready for the day of battle, but victory belongs to the Lord," This verse acknowledges that we can prepare and strive for victory, but ultimately, it is God who grants success.

Romans 8:37: "But in all these things we are more than conquerors through him who loved us." This verse assures believers that they are more than conquerors because of God's love and power, not their own strength.

1 Corinthians 15:57:"But thanks be to God, who gives us the victory through our Lord Jesus Christ." This verse attributes victory to God's grace through Christ, emphasizing that it is not a result of our own efforts.

Philippians 4:13:"I can do all things through Christ who strengthens me." This verse highlights the power of Christ to empower believers to overcome challenges and achieve victory, emphasizing that our strength comes from God, not from ourselves.

Understanding Potential Disruptions:

Proverbs 3:5-6: "Trust in the Lord with all thine heart; and lean not to thine own understanding. In all thy ways acknowledge him, and he shall direct thy paths." This verse warns against relying on our own understanding and emphasizes the importance of seeking God's guidance in all matters.

2 Corinthians 10:4:"For the weapons of our warfare are not carnal, but mighty through God to the pulling down of strongholds." This verse highlights that our spiritual warfare relies on God's power, not our own, and emphasizes the importance of relying on God's strength.

Implementing Measures to Counteract Forces:

Matthew 6:33:"But seek first his kingdom and his righteousness, and all these things will be added to you." This verse encourages believers to prioritize God's will and trust in his provision, rather than striving for earthly success through self-reliance.

Ephesians 6:12:"For our struggle is not against enemies of flesh and blood, but against the rulers, against the authorities, against the powers of this dark world and against the spiritual forces of evil in the heavenly realms." This verse acknowledges the spiritual battle we face and emphasizes the need to rely on God's armor and strength.

Psalm 56:3:"When I am afraid, I will trust in you." This verse encourages believers to turn to God in times of fear and difficulty, trusting in his protection and guidance.

In essence, the Bible teaches that while we may strive for success and victory, true achievement and lasting peace come from trusting in God's power and relying on his guidance, rather than our own strength or understanding. By acknowledging our limitations and seeking God's help, we can experience true and enduring victory in all aspects of life.

Living as Overcomers

In the pursuit of overcoming challenges and adversities, it is crucial to understand the dynamics of living victoriously. This journey involves a fundamental shift in perspective, focusing on the promises and faithfulness of God rather than the daunting circumstances that often confront us. The key lies in recognizing that every trial and tribulation is not merely an obstacle but an opportunity for growth and deeper reliance on divine strength.

Several Bible verses emphasize that trials and tribulations, while difficult, are opportunities for spiritual growth and reliance on God's strength. Key passages include Romans 5:3-5, James 1:2-4, and James 1:12, which highlight the development of endurance, character, and hope through suffering.

The essence of living as overcomers is embedded in the ability to replace stress with peace. When faced with adversities, instead of succumbing to stress, one must channel their focus towards the unwavering faithfulness of God (Lamentations 3:22-23). This involves a conscious decision to let Christ's peace guard the heart and mind, ensuring that anxiety does not take root (Philippians 4:6-7). It is this steadfast focus on divine faithfulness that cultivates an inner peace, even amidst turmoil.

Rejoicing in the face of trials is another significant aspect. It may seem counterintuitive to find joy during hardships, yet it is precisely this attitude that transforms the nature of our experiences. By viewing challenges as a participation in the sufferings of Christ, believers can find a profound joy that transcends temporary discomforts. This joy is not derived from the circumstances themselves, but from the assurance that God found in His living words, is working through them for a greater purpose.

A crucial strategy in overcoming life's challenges is to shift focus from the immediate circumstances to the eternal truths found in God's word. This shift requires a deliberate effort to lay aside every weight and sin that entangles, allowing believers to run with perseverance the race marked out for them (Hebrew 12:1). By fixing their eyes on Jesus, the author and perfecter of faith, individuals can draw strength and courage to endure and overcome (Hebrew 12:2).

Moreover, resisting adversarial attacks is essential (James 4:7, Ephesian 6:11). Victory is not a passive experience but an active endeavor that involves utilizing the spiritual armor and weapons provided by God (Ephesian 6"10-18). This includes resisting negative thoughts and casting evil forces out in the name of Jesus, thereby preventing them from taking hold in the mind and heart.

Releasing faith plays a pivotal role in this journey of overcoming. It involves casting all cares upon Jesus, trusting fully in His promises, and acting as though the resolution is already accomplished. This unwavering faith, free from doubt, is the cornerstone of receiving God's promises and experiencing victory in every circumstance.

Ultimately, living as overcomers means persevering through trials with a spirit of endurance. It requires a commitment to remain steadfast in prayer and faith, expecting divine intervention and deliverance. Romans 12:12 and Colossians 4:2-6 encourage believers to be "constant in prayer" and "watchful in it with thanksgiving," highlighting the importance of persistent prayer. This perseverance is rewarded with the crown of life promised to those who endure. By embracing these principles, believers can break free from cycles of defeat and step into a life marked by victory and fulfillment in God's promises.

The Cycle of Triumph

In the realm of spiritual battles, the concept of triumph is not merely an abstract ideal but a tangible reality that believers can attain. Triumph, in this context, is characterized by the ability to rise above the adversities and challenges orchestrated by Satan. This cycle of triumph is built upon foundational truths that empower individuals to break free from the constraints of defeat and embrace a life of victory.

At the core of this cycle is the understanding that God's ultimate purpose is to do good for His people (Roman 8:28-29). Regardless of the trials faced, believers can rest assured that these are not meant to harm but to refine and strengthen (James 1:2-4). This perspective transforms how challenges are perceived, shifting the focus from the immediacy of pain to the long-term benefits of spiritual growth and maturity.

One pivotal aspect of living in triumph is recognizing the sovereignty of God over all circumstances. Satan's influence is limited, and he requires permission to affect any aspect of a believer's life (Job 1:9-11). This truth provides a profound sense of security; knowing that nothing occurs outside of God's will allows believers to face trials with confidence and peace. Moreover, this assurance fosters a mindset that is not easily shaken by the adversities of life.

With every challenge, there is an accompanying provision for victory. God, in His wisdom, ensures that each trial is not only bearable but also purposeful. The trials are designed to build endurance, leading believers to a place of completeness and maturity, devoid of any deficiencies (James 1:2-4). This divine provision acts as a beacon of hope, guiding believers through the darkest times with the promise of triumph.

To successfully navigate this cycle of triumph, believers must engage actively in spiritual warfare. This involves resisting Satan's attempts to instill fear, doubt, and worry (Ephesian 6:11-18). It requires a conscious effort to focus on God's promises and to utilize the spiritual armor provided for protection and offense as per Ephesian 6:11-18. By doing so, believers can thwart Satan's strategies and maintain their position of victory.

Faith plays a critical role in this cycle. It is through faith that believers can claim and act upon God's promises, even before the evidence of victory is visible. This faith is not passive but a dynamic force that requires believers to act as though the victory is already theirs. It involves casting all anxieties upon God (1 Peter 5:7), trusting in His covenant promises (Hebrew 10:23), and living in the reality of His provision (Philippines 4:19).

Perseverance is another vital component (James 1:12). The journey to triumph is often long and fraught with obstacles. However, those who persevere in faith, prayer, and obedience will inevitably see the fulfillment of God's promises. This perseverance is not a mere endurance of hardship but an active engagement with God's will, continually expecting His deliverance.

Ultimately, the cycle of triumph is a testament to God's faithfulness 2 Thessalonians 3:3). It is about shifting from a mindset of defeat to one of victory (1 Corinthians 15:57), where every circumstance is seen as an opportunity for growth and testimony to God's power (Roman 8:28). Through understanding, faith, and perseverance, believers can transcend the cycle of defeat and live in the perpetual victory that God has ordained for them in Christ.

13

Embracing a New Life

The Promise of Renewal

In the midst of life's challenges, there lies a profound promise of God that speaks to the heart of transformation and hope. This promise is not merely a fleeting wish but a substantial assurance that renewal is possible even when circumstances seem dire. The essence of this promise lies in understanding that life's trials are not designed to defeat us but to build resilience and fortitude. It is about shifting our perspective from one of defeat to one of victory in Christ already achieved, recognizing that within every hardship lies the potential for growth and renewal (Romans 5:3-5).

The first step towards embracing this promise is to recognize that stress and anxiety are not the end of the story. They are, instead, opportunities to cultivate peace and trust in a on Sovereign God. By shifting focus from the overwhelming nature of trials to the steadfastness of divine faithfulness of sovereign God, one can find a peace that transcends understanding (Philippians 4:7). This peace acts as a guard over our hearts and minds, ensuring that we are not swayed by the storms of life but are anchored in a deeper sense of purpose and calm.

Furthermore, the promise of renewal invites us to rejoice even in the face of trials. This rejoicing is not a denial of reality but a profound act of faith on sovereign God that acknowledges the presence of a greater plan at work. It is about finding joy in the assurance that we are not alone and that the trials we face are not in vain. This joy is a testament to the strength we gain through adversity and the character that is forged in the fires of tribulation.

Another critical aspect of this promise is the call to shift our gaze from our immediate circumstances to the broader narrative of faith and purpose. By focusing on the eternal rather than the temporal, we are empowered to navigate life's challenges with a renewed sense of hope and determination. This shift in perspective allows us to see beyond the immediate pain and to trust in the unfolding of a divine plan that promises good even in the midst of difficulty.

Moreover, the promise of renewal is a call to action. It is an invitation to actively resist the forces (James 4:7) that seek to keep us in a cycle of defeat. By donning the armor of faith and wielding the weapons of spiritual warfare (Ephesian 6:10-18), we are equipped to stand firm against any adversity. This active resistance is not about fighting in our strength but about drawing on the divine strength that is promised to us in the word of God, ensuring that we remain unshaken and victorious.

Finally, this promise is about releasing our faith in the face of uncertainty. It is about casting our cares upon sovereign God and trusting that every need will be met according to divine riches and glory (Philippines 4:19). This act of faith is a declaration of our trust in the promises made to us, knowing that they are true and reliable (2 Corinthians 2:20). It is in this release that we find the freedom to live victoriously, even in the midst of life's most challenging circumstances.

Living with Purpose

Living with purpose involves understanding the significance of aligning oneself with a deeper meaning that transcends daily challenges. The concept emphasizes that each individual has a unique role to play, designed by divine intention. Recognizing this purpose is crucial in overcoming feelings of defeat and helplessness that often arise from life's adversities.

The journey to discovering one's purpose starts with introspection and faith. It requires a conscious effort to shift focus from external circumstances to internal reflection. This shift allows individuals to connect with their inner selves and understand the divine plan for their lives. In doing so, they can find peace and resilience, knowing that their struggles are not in vain but are part of a larger, beneficial design.

A key aspect of living with purpose is the belief that God is in control of all circumstances (Isaiah 32:18). This belief provides a foundation of stability, as it reassures individuals that their trials are not random or meaningless. Instead, these experiences are opportunities for growth and development, tailored to enhance their character and faith (James 1:2-4). By embracing this perspective, individuals can transform challenges into stepping stones towards spiritual maturity and fulfillment.

Moreover, living with purpose involves actively resisting negative influences pushed in the mind by the power of darkness or brought through people or circumstance that aim to derail one's spiritual journey. It requires vigilance and the use of spiritual tools / armors, such as prayer and meditation, to combat doubt and fear. By keeping faith at the forefront, individuals can maintain clarity and focus, even in the face of adversity. This proactive approach ensures that they remain aligned with their divine purpose, enabling them to navigate life's complexities with confidence and grace.

Another important element is the understanding that purpose is not static but evolves with time and experience. As individuals grow and learn, their purpose may expand or change, reflecting new insights and understanding. This dynamic nature of purpose encourages continuous learning and adaptation, fostering a sense of curiosity and openness to new possibilities. It underscores the importance of remaining flexible and receptive to change, as this adaptability is crucial for personal and spiritual growth.

In essence, living with purpose is about finding meaning in every aspect of life. It is about recognizing the interconnectedness of all experiences and understanding that each moment is a part of a larger, divine narrative. This awareness brings a sense of peace and fulfillment, as individuals realize that they are part of something greater than themselves. By embracing this mindset, they can break free from the cycle of defeat and step into a life of purpose and victory.

Ultimately, living with purpose is a transformative journey that empowers individuals to rise above their circumstances. It instills a sense of hope and direction, guiding them towards a life of meaning and impact. Through faith and perseverance, individuals can uncover their true calling and live in alignment with the divine purpose of sovereign God intended for them, leading to a life of joy, peace, and fulfillment.

Transforming Circumstances

In the realm of life's challenges, the concept of transforming circumstances emerges as a pivotal strategy to break the cycle of defeat. This process involves a deliberate shift in perspective and action, enabling individuals to harness their situations for growth and victory rather than succumbing to defeat. The foundational step in this transformation is to replace stress with peace. When adversities arise, instead of allowing stress to dominate, one is encouraged to focus on a divine faithfulness found in the living word of God, allowing peace to guard the heart and mind. This peace is not passive but an active choice to trust in a higher strength, which provides a stable foundation amidst chaos.

Another crucial element is the act of rejoicing, even in trials. This counterintuitive approach is rooted in the understanding that trials are not mere obstacles but opportunities for deeper participation in a greater purpose. The act of rejoicing transforms the perception of trials, acknowledging them as part of a larger narrative where ultimate good is being worked out. It is about maintaining a posture of praise, not for the trials themselves, but for the presence and purpose they reveal.

Central to transforming circumstances is the redirection of focus from the problem to a higher perspective. This involves a conscious decision to fix one's eyes not on the immediate challenges but on enduring truths and promises of God. This shift in focus is akin to looking beyond the horizon of current struggles to the broader landscape of purpose and possibility. It requires a steadfast commitment to a vision that transcends present difficulties.

Resisting negative influences is another vital aspect of transformation. Life's challenges often come with a barrage of fear, doubt, and worry. Here, the importance of resistance is emphasized—not through sheer willpower alone, but through a reliance on spiritual armor and weapons designed for such battles as per Ephesian 6:10-18. This resistance is not passive but involves an active engagement with the forces of darkness that seek to undermine one's peace and purpose.

Finally, the release of faith plays a critical role in transforming circumstances. This involves casting all cares and concerns onto a trustworthy source (1 Peter 5:7). It's an act of faith that moves beyond intellectual assent to a lived reality, where belief is demonstrated through action. This release is not a denial of reality but a profound trust in promises that transcend immediate evidence. By acting on this belief, individuals begin to live as though the answers to their prayers are already in motion.

Through these steps, the cycle of defeat is broken, and a new cycle of victory is established. This transformation is not a one-time event but a continuous process of aligning one's life with principles that foster resilience and hope through the word of God. By engaging with these transformative practices, individuals can navigate their circumstances with confidence, knowing that each challenge is an opportunity for growth and victory.

A Life of Victory

In the pursuit of a victorious life, it is crucial to understand the dynamics of overcoming the cycle of defeat. This cycle is often perpetuated by the adversities the devil and challenges that life presents, and it is a common experience for many Christians. However, the key to breaking free from this cycle lies in recognizing and utilizing the provisions that are inherently available in every trial. These provisions are not mere escape routes but are opportunities for growth, endurance, and ultimate victory.

Firstly, it is essential to acknowledge that every circumstance, no matter how dire, comes with a divine provision for victory. This understanding transforms the perspective from one of despair to one of hope and resilience. By focusing not on the problem but on the possibilities, it presents, individuals can harness the strength needed to overcome. This mindset shift is pivotal in moving from a state of defeat to one of victory.

Moreover, it is important to maintain a steadfast focus on the bigger picture, which is often obscured by immediate challenges. By keeping one's eyes fixed on the ultimate goal of victory, and by trusting in the divine plan that orchestrates every event in life for good, the cycle of defeat can be dismantled. This requires a conscious effort to look beyond the present trials and to have faith in the unseen outcomes that promise fulfillment and triumph.

In addition to perspective and focus, action plays a crucial role. It is not enough to merely believe in victory; one must also actively pursue it through faith-driven actions. This involves resisting the temptation to succumb to fear, worry, and doubt, which are tools often used to keep individuals trapped in defeat. Instead, by taking proactive steps to address challenges head-on, and by leveraging the spiritual resources available, a path to victory is paved.

Furthermore, the importance of community and support cannot be understated. Engaging with a community that shares the vision of victory provides encouragement and reinforcement. This collective strength is instrumental in overcoming the isolation that often accompanies defeat.

Together, individuals can share insights, offer support, and celebrate victories, reinforcing the cycle of victory instead of defeat.

Finally, the journey to a life of victory is not a solitary endeavor but a partnership with the divine, sovereign God through Christ. By aligning one's will with his divine purpose and by seeking guidance and strength from a him, individuals are empowered to overcome any obstacle. This divine partnership ensures that no challenge is insurmountable and that victory is not just a possibility, but a promise.

Keep Going: - But our consummate victory over the devil and all his angels was not accomplished by us or our power. Christ had complete victory over Satan. He is the "Strong Man" who bound and captured the devil, stripped him of his armor, and plundered him of his possessions (Luke 11:20–22; Colossians 2:15; Hebrews 2:14; 1 John 3:8). It is Christ's victory that we share and participate in.

So never be discouraged. If you stumble, get up and march on with Jesus. If you give in to temptation, confess it to God and continue to follow Jesus. And if you fall a million times and seem to lose multiple battles, don't despair. Christ has already won the battle over Satan, sin, the world, and death. Keep clinging to Jesus and He will place your feet on rock so that you slip not. Keep believing in Him. "This is the victory that overcomes the world, even our faith. Who is it that overcomes the world? Only the one who believes that Jesus is the Son of God" (1 John 5:4–5).

In conclusion, living a life of victory is attainable through a combination of perspective, focus, action, community, and divine partnership. By embracing these elements, the cycle of defeat is broken, and a new cycle of victory is established, leading to a fulfilling and triumphant life.

My prayer: -

Since you have finished the book and it is my prayer to you that may the Lord Jesus, strengthen you and help you to trust on Him from beginning to end during this journey of faith based on the insights received through this book. May the Lord help you to keep you focused upon Him, the author and perfecter of faith. No matter how many times you have failed, may the Lord Jesus help you to grasp the truth, found in His words and enable you to experience your consummate victory in heaven.

Amen.